S0-BNS-118

# *Computers as Theatre*

# *Computers as Theatre*

Brenda Laurel

**Addison-Wesley Publishing Company**
Reading, Massachusetts • Menlo Park, California • New York
Don Mills, Ontario • Wokingham, England • Amsterdam • Bonn
Sydney • Singapore • Tokyo • Madrid • San Juan • Milan • Paris

*Sponsoring Editor:* Peter S. Gordon
*Production Administrator:* Sarah Hallet
*Production Assistant:* Genevra Hanke
*Cover Design:* Jean Seal
*Insert Design:* C. J. Petlick, Hunter Graphics
*Copyeditor:* Stephanie Argeros-Magean
*Electronic Production Administrator:* Beth Perry
*Manufacturing Manager:* Roy Logan
*Senior Manufacturing Coordinator:* Judy Sullivan



Library of Congress Cataloging-in-Publication Data

Laurel, Brenda.
Computers as theatre / Brenda Laurel.
p. cm.
Includes bibliographical references and index.
ISBN 0-201-51048-0
1. Human-computer interaction. 2. User interfaces (Computer systems) I. Title.
QA76.9.H85L38 1991
005.2—dc20 90-24953
CIP



Reprinted with corrections November, 1991



2 3 4 5 6 7 8 9 10-DO-9594939291

This book is dedicated to my mother
and
to the memory of my father,
who showed me that work, love, and values
all arise from the same source.

# *Contents*

# Foreword

> Movies did not flourish until the engineers lost control to artists—or more precisely, to the communications craftsmen. The same thing is happening now with personal computers.[1]
>
> Think of the computer, not as a tool, but as a medium.[2]

This is a challenging book, one that offers an entirely new perspective upon the development of the modern technologies of computation and communication. The main theme of this multithemed book is that these technologies offer new opportunities for creative, interactive experiences and, in particular, for new forms of drama. But these new opportunities will come to pass only if control of the technology is taken from the technologist and given to those who understand human beings, human interaction, communication, pleasure, and pain.

It is time for the engineers to go back to engineering. To develop these new technologies, we need a new breed of creative individuals, most likely those associated with poetry, writing, and theatrical direction. Who, asks Laurel, who better understands human interaction than the dramatist? The dramatic arts have a tradition of several thousand years in thought, study, and experimentation with human experience and with a variety of modes of interaction. Today, in the absence of informed guidance, we stumble toward a new technological era made possible by the emerging technolo-

---

[1]From P. Heckel, *The Elements of Friendly Software Design*. New York: Warner Books, 1984, p. 5.
[2]From B. Laurel, *Computers as Theatre*, Chapter 5.

gies of the computer, video, telephone, and high-quality sound.

Alas, the stumbling is not guided by any understanding of the nature of interaction. Instead, it is more like the tale describing the groping of those legendary blind men touching an elephant. Not only does each "explorer" have a different understanding of what kind of beast this elephant might be, but there is no interaction among them, no way in which they can make sense of their individual experiences.

Evidence of both the new technologies and of our many stumbles is all about us—from the automatic bank tellers, "programmable" ovens, video recorders, and thermostats that confuse our daily lives, to the plethora of office programs that are starting to dominate our business lives.

The key word in finding an illuminating path through the technological maze is "interaction." These new technologies all have one thing in common: They can aid our interaction with others, with knowledge, information, and experience, and even with the devices themselves. When we look toward what is known about the nature of interaction, why not turn to those who manage it best—to those from the world of drama, of the stage, of the theatre?

Today, the technology is provided by the technologists. It is, therefore, no wonder that most new devices, including computers and their software applications emphasize technology over all else. Each program or device comes with multiple "features," new complexities to learn, new functions that can be performed. Even the games sired by these new technologies emphasize technological aspects over dramatic them, adding sounds and colors, motion and spectacle all in the service of technology that amazes and astounds.

Do you enjoy the experience of using these new technologies? If not, why not? perhaps it never even occurred to you that the concepts of "enjoy" or "experience" could apply to the new devices, with perhaps the exception of the television set or the game whose functions are, after all, to entertain. But shouldn't you? After all, the purpose of most of these technologies is to assist us in doing our daily activities, perhaps providing new tools or new approaches. And we most certainly should enjoy the experience of doing those activities.

This is a book to lead to reflection and pondering, especially if you are one of those folks involved in the development of new technologies but also if you are one of the vast majority who simply suffers. To appreciate this book fully requires some knowledge of theatre and art, of new emerging technologies, and of computer games. But most of all, it requires an open and imaginative mind. The lessons of the book are clear: There is much to learn from theatre. Application of those lessons is not so clear—perhaps being best left as real, practical exercises for the readers.

In a theatrical performance, we expect to have a beginning, a middle, and an end. There should be a purpose or goal to the activities, and events should all be understandable with respect to some underlying theme or motif. Theatrical interaction has peaks and valleys, perhaps even expressed by means of a graph that starts low, peaks at the climax of the occasion, and then comes back down to a graceful conclusion. We can all understand how such a description makes sense for a theatrical performance, or even for a computer game. But what about for more mundane tasks: Mowing the lawn? Writing an interoffice memo? Balancing a checkbook or other account? Making up a shopping list? Why would we expect to see some sense of excitement in these activities? Where is the climax to a checkbook or shopping list?

But to ask these questions about those tasks is to miss the spirit of the book. Sure, we will always have those kinds of things to do, and sure, nothing is going to turn those activities into soaring drama. But maybe, just maybe, if we take the lessons of this book seriously, we will take a much larger, much higher view of human activities. Maybe the unit is the day, from the slow waking up in the morning, to the discovery of the day's events, to some major fulfilling activity, to a slow tapering off and resolution that enables us to end gracefully and fall asleep comfortable. Maybe the unit is an office group, working on a project from inception to completion, with peak moments of experience in the midst that determine the success or failure of the project.

We need to view each of our activities in a larger framework. Then each single device can be built in a way that makes sense within the whole framework of the day or task, so that each device can fit gracefully into its place in the total activity and add to our enhancement of the task.

Some of you who work in the field called "human-computer interaction" may be disappointed at first reading. You may miss controlled studies and specific specifications. You will not find anything you can apply to your work today, or even tomorrow. You will have to think of characters and "points of view." And some of the most advanced notions of today are challenged and replaced.

For example, the three major emphases in current modern computer system design can be summarized as follows:

- Design consistent objects and environments.
- Develop a metaphor for the task, tools, and actions and make all activities consistent with that metaphor.
- Think of the computer as a tool.

Now consider three of Laurel's "Rules of Thumb," discussed in Chapter 5:

- Focus on designing the action. The design of objects, environments, and characters is all subsidiary to this central goal.
- Interface metaphors have limited usefulness. What you gain now you may have to pay for later.
- Think of the computer not as a tool, but as a medium.

The current emphases make sense in today's context where design is for the small, for self-contained minute-by-minute activities. But Laurel has a more cohesive goal in mind. She emphasizes that which is large, the totality where activities are intertwined with one another, where each individual activity makes sense only when viewed with respect to the others, and where the whole set may be of considerable duration. Laurel is concerned with the total experience. If new technologies are to enhance that experience, they must be designed to take that larger, more global view.

This book will challenge you to think about new concepts and new approaches. The theme is to go beyond that which was possible until now. To think of human interaction as drama is to think broadly, to take a wide overview, and to emphasize the thematic aspects of our daily activities and needs. By so doing, we free ourselves from small, mundane considerations. Most importantly of all, this book forces us to take a wider, broader perspective on the nature of human activity. Technology can enrich our experience and increase our enjoyment, but only if properly conceived and properly applied.

Donald A. Norman
*University of California, San Diego*

# Preface

This book presents a dramatic theory of human-computer activity. Usually, we think about interactive computing in terms of two things: an application and an interface. In the reigning view, these two things are conceptually distinct: An application provides specific functionality for specific goals, and an interface represents that functionality to people. The interface is the thing that we communicate with—the thing we "talk" to—the thing that mediates between us and the inner workings of the machine. The interface is typically designed last, after the application is thoroughly conceived and perhaps even implemented; it is attached to a preexisting bundle of "functionality" to serve as its contact surface.

This way of thinking about human-computer activity has strongly influenced the discipline of interface design. It loads the interface with responsibility for all aspects of a person's experience with a computer—sensory, cognitive, and emotional. A scientific approach dominates the design of human-computer interaction today. Such disciplines as cognitive psychology, ergonomics, and optics have been drawn in to support computer scientists in the task of designing interfaces for their applications. More recently, graphic and sound design have been introduced into the interdisciplinary mix. Although these artistic disciplines have gained some acceptance as elements of good design, contemporary design *practice* typically accommodates the arts as something fundamentally alien to the computer landscape.

Certain problems in the design of human-computer activity seem particularly intractable in terms of "mainstream" interface theory. What do we do about the feeling that people often have that their access to the functionality of an application is limited, mediated, or even obstructed by its interface? People often resent the limitations interfaces place on their behavior, but how can we predispose people to make functional and appropriate choices without explicit constraints? People are often distracted by the need to "figure out" and "negotiate with" interfaces—how can we eliminate this sense of indirection? What can we do about the little cognitive train wrecks that occur at the interstices between modes in a drawing program, a word processor, or a virtual-reality system? The hand wavers between the keyboard and mouse button, and the mind, even though it is working thousands of times faster and more elegantly than the computer itself, cannot predict the behavior of the interface. There is the overwhelming sense of something being in the way, something standing between us and what we are trying to do.

Direct-manipulation systems, like the Macintosh desktop, attempt to bridge the interface gulf by representing the world of the computer as a collection of objects that are directly analogous to objects in the real world. But the complex and abundant functionality of today's new applications—which parallels people's rising expectations about what they might accomplish with computers—threatens to push us over the edge of the metaphorical desktop. The power of the computer is locked behind a door with no knob.

A complement to the notion of direct manipulation is the idea of direct engagement. It shifts the focus from the representation of manipulable objects to the ideal of enabling people to engage directly in the activity of choice, whether it be manipulating symbolic tools in the performance of some instrumental task or wandering around the imaginary world of a computer game. Direct engagement emphasizes emotional as well as cognitive values. It conceives of human-computer activity as *designed experience*, and it reconfigures the design of applications and interfaces as a single integrated process.

The notion of direct engagement opens the door to artistic considerations that are broader than the aesthetics of screen design. Unlike a strictly scientific approach, the notion of designed experience leads to a design discipline in which ideas like *pleasure* and *engagement* are not only appropriate but attainable. It emphasizes the intrinsically interdisciplinary nature of design by blurring the edges between application and interface and by incorporating insights and techniques from artistic disciplines, especially drama and theatre. By simply changing their vantage point, designers steeped in computer science and traditional interface theory may discover rich new sources of theoretical and productive knowledge that can be brought to bear on the design of human-computer activity.

Adopting a point of view that is relatively more "artistic" than "scientific" does not mean that logic, specificity, or disciplined thinking must be abandoned—quite the contrary. The first half of this book presents a general theory that can be described as a *poetics* of human-computer activity. It employs an analysis of the nature and uses of human-computer activity to extend and modify the theory of literary representations presented in Aristotle's *Poetics*. The *Poetics* defines form and structure in drama and narrative literature and provides an understanding of how structural elements can be combined to create organic wholes. Its uses are both critical (understanding how such representations work) and productive (how to make them). This book likewise attempts to provide a comprehensive theory of form and structure for representations in which both humans and computers participate. By examining the world of human-computer activity with the same rigor and logic as Aristotle applied to the literary arts, we can arrive at a set of principles that may provide greater acuity, robustness, and elegance than the piecemeal science that often guides the design of human-computer activity.

Roughly the second half of this book explores some of the critical and productive implications of the theory in relation to several key topics. The chapters in this section are intended to illustrate the applicability of the general theory in a variety of contexts and to suggest some new design approaches. As well as applying dramatic theory, these chapters draw upon the work of such key researchers and thinkers as Alan Kay, Scott Fisher, Ted Nelson, William Buxton, Chris Schmandt, Susan Brennan, Myron Krueger, and Donald Norman.

This book is written for people who concern themselves explicitly with what people experience while interacting with computers. Human-computer interface design is the "official" discipline that treats these concerns. But the need for a theory of human-computer experience obviously extends beyond the interface community; indeed, a goal of that community is to raise the "interface" consciousness of a much larger population, including software and hardware designers, students of computer science, and builders of interactive technology for a wide spectrum of uses and contexts. Although the book treats subjects that are generally considered to be in the "interface" domain, it is intended to be accessible and useful to designers outside the anointed interface community as well.

The only prerequisites for making use of the ideas in this book are some exposure to computers and a sensitivity to people's experiences with them. Readers who are versed in "traditional" interface theory and technique will have a keener eye for the central issues and controversies that are addressed, but they may expect to encounter a conceptual framework that is in some ways orthogonal to their own. Readers who are familiar with dramatic or literary theory and criticism may be abraded by the systematicity of the theory and its structuralist flavor, but they can expect to discover illuminating connections between their expertise and the world of human-computer activity.

My goal in writing this book is to improve the quality of human-computer experiences through new approaches to their design. I began my computer career in the mid-1970s while I was an actor and graduate student in theatre. From my first job programming interactive fairy tales on a little home computer to my current work in multimedia and virtual-reality systems, I have continually been struck by the relevance of dramatic theory and practice to interactive media. A continuing goal has been to probe, understand, and explain these connections, to test my ideas against real-world experience with computers as a designer and as a participant, and to embody them in the form of a theory that could be valuable across the whole spectrum of interactive applications and media. Whether you are designing an interface, an application, a computer game, a public-access installation, or a marketing plan, it is my hope that this book can give you a powerful new point of view.[1]

Fundamentally, this book is meant to give its readers *a new place to stand* when considering the design of human-computer activity. It offers a new way to approach problems for which traditional methods offer no clear solution. It provides designers with a conceptual framework and a vocabulary that are strongly focused on human experience. It will enable interactivity designers to tap into the vast storehouse of dramatic theory and technique. Hopefully, it will lead to the design of human-computer activities that are more usable, understandable, and engaging. Ultimately, the theory and techniques in this book may help to create new visions of what people can do with computers.

---

[1]As Alan Kay once said, "Point of view is worth 80 IQ points."

# Acknowledgments

The writing of this book was an exercise in patience, nurturing, and dogged but gentle argument for many of my friends and colleagues over many years. It represents not only my own work and obsessions, but also a decade of collaboration with a great many people.

First, I must thank those who gave me my start in interactive media. My old friend and theatrical collaborator William Morton introduced me to the virtual-reality aspects of theatre back in the early 1970s. Joe Miller, the first bona fide computer wizard of my acquaintance, dragged me kicking and screaming into the world of programming and design, helping me to find ways to augment and work around my nearly absent background in mathematics. Joe and the rest of the gang at CyberVision—John and Janey Powers, Jeffrey Schwamberger, and Ken and Eiko Balthaser—have been a continuing source of ideas and encouragement since the late 1970s. I am also extremely grateful to Don Glancy, my doctoral advisor, for embedding Aristotle in my brain, teaching me to write, and encouraging me to go beyond the traditional boundaries of dramatic criticism.

My early Atari experiences were enriched by contact with blue-sky specialists Stephen Arnold, Clyde Grossman, Ted Kahn, Ed Rotberg, and Greg Weiner. The remarkable group at the Atari Systems Research Laboratory (1982–1984; RIP) induced violently pleasurable tectonic activity in my thinking. Thanks first to Alan Kay for rescuing me from the world of suits and giving me a chance to do some "real" research. Thanks also to all of the members of the research staff, including Susan Brennan, Doug Crockford, Jim Dunion, Steve Gano, and Kristina Hooper, and to lab associates

Douglas Adams, Ray Bradbury, Doug Lenat, and Margaret Minsky. Special thanks to Howard Rheingold for crystalizing much of our thinking at the Atari Lab in his book, *Tools for Thought*, and also for his abiding friendship and advice as a veteran writer. I have also been graced by occasional mind-blowing conversations with Nicholas Negroponte, no doubt by virtue of my status as a Media Lab groupie. Michael Naimark, Don Norman, and Rachel Strickland have remained invaluable collaborators since the Atari Lab days and have had a huge impact on my thinking.

Since Atari, the game design community (to which I also belong, primarily by force of will) has also provided constant stimulation and collaboration. I am extremely grateful for the insights offered by Chris Crawford, Tim Brengle, Michael Feinberg, David Graves, Jim Gasperini, Ron Martinez, Tom Snyder, and Rob Swigart. My work in interface design and multimedia has been greatly enriched through my associations with Abbe Don, Kristee Kreitman, Tim Oren, David Nagel, and the Apple Human Interface Group. The burgeoning discourse of telepresence has brought me into contact with some of the brightest people and most provocative ideas I have ever encountered, especially William Bricken (who was also at the Atari Lab), Joseph Bates of Carnegie Mellon University, Warren Robinett, Joe Rosen, Sally Rosenthal, Allucquere Stone, William Gibson, and Timothy Leary.

Several people made contributions above and beyond the call of duty to the preparation of this book, including Walter Bender, Allen Cypher, William Gaver, Robert Trappl, Julian Hilton, Myron Krueger, Don Norman, Chris Schmandt, and Ben Shneiderman. Linda O'Brien and Helen Goldstein proved to me once again the value of Addison-Wesley as a publisher. My editor, Peter Gordon, provided motivation and encouragement bordering on the threshold of pain throughout the process.

Deepest thanks to the people in my ad hoc family who have braved the storm of this adventure and who have helped me beyond my ability to thank them. During his too-short life, Bob Perry taught me to dance and dream of spaces filled with endless celebrations. Linda Thornburg endured countless verbal barrages and ended up teaching me to break china at key moments. Brooke Battles handled details, big ideas, small children, and vast quantities of wine with equal ease. I also owe a special debt to my mentor and collaborator in the world of telepresence, Scott Fisher. Scott has shown me a glimpse of what is technologically possible; he has proven that an artist can be a technologist and vice versa, and he has shattered the window that used to frame all of my imaginings about virtual worlds.

To my children, Hilary and Brooke, I owe both thanks for their iridescent imaginations and apologies for the months during which my gaze was locked on the computer screen. My husband Eric Hulteen has been with me continually, through every idea, every sentence, every household disaster, every intractable application, and every messy emotion through the whole process. If anybody buys this book, I intend to let him break a bottle of champagne over my head.

Lots of people contributed help or inspiration for this book. Several are pictured on the front cover, participating in an interface experience. They include: 1. Hilary Laurel Hulteen, 2. Sally Rosenthal, 3. Scott Fisher, 4. Rachel Strickland, 5. Eric Hulteen, 6. Brooke Laurel Hulteen, 7. Brenda Laurel, 8. Steve Gano, 9. Kristee Rosendhal, 10. Brooke Battles, 11. Michael Naimark, 12. Jim Gasperini, 13. Jeff Schwamberger, 14. Ken Balthaser, 15. Lucinda Sahm, 16. Tim Oren, 17. Elaine deLorimier, 18. Michael deLorimier, and 19. John Powers.

Arriving in time for the second feature were (clockwise from left): William Gibson, John Perry Barlow, and Dr. Timothy Leary.

# Computers as Theatre

Chapter One

# The Nature of the Beast

## Representing Action

In 1962, the first computer game was invented by some hackers at MIT. It was called *Spacewar* and it ran on a DEC PDP-1, the world's first minicomputer, connected to a CRT display. One of the game's designers explained that the game was born when a group sat around trying to figure out "what would be interesting displays" they could create for the CRT with some pattern-generating software they had developed. "We decided that probably, you could make a two-dimensional maneuvering sort of thing, and decided that naturally the obvious thing to do was spaceships." The MIT hackers weren't the only ones to invent *Spacewar.* As Alan Kay noted, "the game of *Spacewar* blossoms spontaneously wherever there is a graphics display connected to a computer" [Brand, 1974].

Why was *Spacewar* the "natural" thing to build with this new technology? Why not a pie chart or an automated kaleidoscope or a desktop? Its designers identified *action* as the key ingredient and conceived *Spacewar* as a game that could provide a good balance between thinking and doing for its players. They regarded the computer as a machine naturally suited for representing things that you could see, control, and play with. Its interesting potential lay not in its ability to perform calculations but in its capacity to *represent action in which humans could participate.*

Why don't we look at everything computers do that way? Consider the following question:

**Q:** What is being represented by the Macintosh interface?

1. A desktop.
2. Something that's kind of like a desktop.
3. Someone doing something in an environment that's kind of like a desktop.

Number three is the only answer that comes close. The human is an indispensable ingredient of the representation, since it is only through a person's actions that all dimensions of the representation can be manifest. To put it another way, a computer-based representation without a human participant is like the sound of a tree falling in the proverbial uninhabited forest.

There are two major reasons for belaboring such a seemingly obvious point. First, it wasn't always true—and the design disciplines for applications and interfaces still bear the marks of that former time. Second, reconceptualizing what computers do as representing action with human participants suggests a design philosophy that diverges significantly from much of the contemporary thinking about interfaces.

## *Interface Evolution*

"Interface" has become a trendy (and lucrative) concept over the last several years—a phenomenon that is largely attributable to the introduction of the Apple Macintosh. Interface design is concerned with making computer systems and applications easy to use (or at least usable) by humans. When we think of human-computer interfaces today, we are likely to visualize icons and menu bars, or perhaps command lines and blinking cursors. But it wasn't always so.

John Walker, founder and president of Autodesk, Inc., provides an illuminating account of the "generations" of user interface design [Walker, 1990]. In the beginning, says Walker, there was a one-on-one relationship between a person and a computer through the knobs and dials on the front of massive early machines like the ENIAC. The advent of punch cards and batch processing replaced this direct human-computer interaction with a transaction mediated by a computer operator. Time-sharing and the use of "glass teletypes" reintroduced direct human-computer interaction and led to the command-line and menu-oriented interfaces with which the senior citizens of computing (people over thirty) are probably familiar. Walker attributes the notion of "conversationality" in human-computer interfaces to this kind of interaction, where a person does something and a computer responds—a tit-for-tat interaction.

This simplistic notion of conversation led many early interface specialists to develop a model of interaction that treats human and computer as two distinct parties whose "conversation" is mediated by the screen. But as advances in linguistics have demonstrated, there is more to conversation than tit-for-tat. Dialogue is not just linearized turn-taking in which I say something, you go think about it and then you say something, I go think about it, and so on. An alternative model of conversation employs the notion of *common ground*, described by Herbert H. Clark and Susan E. Brennan [1990]:

> It takes two people working together to play a duet, shake hands, play chess, waltz, teach, or make love. To succeed, the two of them have to coordinate both the content and process of what they are doing. Alan and Barbara, on the piano, must come to play the same Mozart duet. This is coordination of content. They must also synchronize their entrances and exits, coordinate how loud to play forte and pianissimo, and otherwise adjust to each other's tempo and dynamics. This is coordination of process. They cannot even begin to coordinate on content without assuming a vast amount of shared information or common ground—that is, mutual knowledge, mutual beliefs, and mutual assumptions [Clark and Carlson, 1982; Clark and Marshall, 1981; Lewis, 1969; Schelling, 1960]. And to coordinate on process, they need to update, or revise, their common ground moment by moment. All collective actions are built on common ground and its accumulation. [Clark and Brennan, 1990]

In her work in applying the notion of common ground to human-computer interfaces, Brennan [1990a] suggests that common ground is a jointly inhabited "space" where meaning takes shape through the collaboration and successive approximations of the participants. Brennan's ongoing work is aimed at designing human-computer interfaces so that they offer means for establishing common ground ("grounding") that are similar to those that people use in human-to-human conversation—for example, interruptions, questions, utterances, and gestures that indicate whether something is being understood [Brennan, 1990b].

Contemporary graphical interfaces, as exemplified by the Macintosh, explicitly represent part of what is in the "common ground" of interaction through the appearance and behavior of objects on the screen. Some of what goes on in the representation is exclusively attributable to either the person or the computer, and some of what happens is a fortuitous artifact of a collaboration in which the traits, goals, and behaviors of both are inseparably intertwined.

The notion of common ground not only provides a superior representation of the conversational process but also supports the idea that an interface is not simply the means whereby a person and a computer represent themselves to one another; rather it is a shared context for action in which both are agents. (This book will employ the noun "agent" to mean *one who initiates action*, a definition consistent with Aristotle's use of the concept in the *Poetics*. Insurance agents, real estate agents, and secret agents are examples of a kind of agency that is more complex—and vaguely ominous. The subject of "interface agents" is discussed later in Chapter 5.) When the old tit-for-tat paradigm intrudes, the "conversation" is likely to break down, once again relegating person and computer to opposite sides of a "mystic gulf" filled with hidden processes, arbitrary understandings and misunderstandings, and power relationships that are competitive rather than cooperative. "Mistakes," unanticipated outcomes, and error messages are typical evidence of such a breakdown in communication, where the common ground becomes a sea of misunderstanding.

The notion of interface metaphors was introduced to provide people with a conceptual scheme that would guard against such misunderstandings by deploying familiar objects and environments as stakes in the common ground. But even "good" metaphors don't always work. For instance, in an informal survey of Macintosh-literate university students, many people failed to employ the word "desktop" anywhere in their description of the Finder.[1] Where an interface metaphor diverges significantly from its real-world referent, people proceed by accounting for the behaviors of particular "objects" on the screen with ad hoc explanations of system operation, which are often incorrect—a "naive physics" of computing [see Owen 1986]. In such cases, metaphors do not serve as "stakes in the common ground," but rather as cognitive mediators whose labels may be somewhat less arcane (but possibly more ambiguous) than a computer scientist's jargon.

Although interface metaphors can fail in many ways (as discussed later in Chapter 5), their growing prevalence, especially in graphical interfaces, has expanded the domain of interface design to admit contributions from specialists in graphic and industrial design, linguistics, psychology, education, and other disciplines. An important contribution of the metaphorical approach has been to make interface design an *interdisciplinary* concern. The next section focuses on two of those "interdisciplines": psychology and graphic design.

## *Interface Interdisciplines*

Psychology is a familiar domain to dramatists, actors, and other theatre artists because of its focus on human behavior. Understanding how psychology and theatre are alike and

[1]The Macintosh Finder is an application for managing people's file systems and for launching other applications. It comes with the system and is automatically launched when the machine is turned on. The Finder was designed on the basis of a "desktop metaphor," employing graphical icons to represent individual files as "documents" and hierarchical organizational units as "folders."

different may illuminate the distinct contributions that each can make in the field of human-computer interaction.

The two disciplines have several elements in common. Both concern themselves with how agents relate to one another in the process of communicating, solving problems, building things, having fun—the whole range of human activity. Both interpret human behavior in terms of goals, obstacles, conflicts, discoveries, changes of mind, successes, and failures. Both domains have important contributions to make to interface theory and design. Both attempt to observe and understand human behavior, but they employ that understanding to different ends: In general, psychology attempts to *describe what goes on in the real world* with all its fuzziness and loose ends, while theatre attempts to *represent something that might go on*, simplified for the purposes of logical and affective clarity. Psychology is devoted to the end of explaining human behavior, while drama attempts to represent it in a form that provides intellectual and emotional closure. Theatre is informed by psychology (both professional and amateur flavors), but it turns a trick that is outside of psychology's province through the art of representing action. By taking a look at some of the key ideas that psychology has contributed to interface design, we may be able to identify some ways in which theatrical knowledge can extend and complement them.

Psychologists have been involved in the quest to understand and shape human-computer interaction almost since the beginning of computing, through such disciplines as human factors and computer-aided instruction.[2] In the 1970s

---

[2]The literature on "human factors" and other psychological perspectives on human-computer interaction is huge. It is beyond the scope and purpose of this book to provide even a cursory survey of the entire domain. The work mentioned in this chapter is selected in terms of its relevance to the thesis of this particular book. Interested readers may wish to review *The Human Factor: Designing Computer Systems for People* by Richard Rubinstein and Harry Hersh [1984], which includes an excellent bibliography, *Readings in Human-Computer Interaction: A Multidisciplinary Approach* by Ronald M. Baecker and William A.S. Buxton [1987], or the various proceedings of ACM SIGCHI and the Human Factors Society.

and on through the 1980s, cognitive psychologists developed perspectives on human-computer interaction that were more critically focused on interface design than those of their colleagues in other branches of psychology. The work of Donald A. Norman, founder of the Institute for Cognitive Psychology at the University of California at San Diego, is especially illuminating. In the 1980s, Norman built a lab at UCSD that fostered some of the most innovative and germane thinking about human-computer interaction to date [see Norman and Draper, 1986, for a collection of essays by members and associates of this group]. Norman's perspective is highly task-oriented. In his book, *The Psychology of Everyday Things* [1988], Norman drives home the point that the design of an effective interface—whether for a computer or a doorknob—must begin with an analysis of what a person is trying to *do*, rather than with a metaphor or a notion of what the screen should display.

Norman's emphasis on action as the stuff that interfaces both *enable* and *represent* bores a tunnel out of the labyrinth of metaphor and brings us back out into the light, where *what is going on* is larger, more complex, and more fundamental than the way the human and the computer "talk" to each other about it.

Norman's insights dovetail nicely with those of the "common ground" linguists, suggesting a notion of the interface that is more than screen-deep. The interface becomes the arena for the performance of some task in which both human and computer have a role. What is represented in the interface is not only the task's environment and tools but also the process of interaction—the contributions made by both parties and evidence of the task's evolution. I believe that Norman's analysis supports the view that interface design should concern itself with representing *whole actions with multiple agents.* This is, by the way, precisely the definition of theatre.

Norman has also been a key figure in the development of another pivotal interface concept, the idea of *direct manipulation.* Direct manipulation interfaces employ a psychologist's knowledge of how people relate to objects in the real world in the belief that people can carry that knowledge across to the manipulation of virtual[3] objects that represent computational entities and processes.

The term *direct manipulation* was coined by Ben Shneiderman of the University of Maryland, who listed three key criteria:

1. Continuous representation of the object of interest.
2. Physical actions or labeled button presses instead of complex syntax.
3. Rapid incremental reversible operations whose impact on the object of interest is immediately visible [Shneiderman, 1987].

Shneiderman reports that direct-manipulation interfaces can "generate a glowing enthusiasm among users that is in marked contrast with the more common reaction of grudging acceptance or outright hostility" [Shneiderman, 1987]. In a cognitive analysis of how direct manipulation works, Hutchins, Hollan, and Norman [1986] suggest that direct manipulation as defined may provide only a partial explanation of such positive feelings. They posit a companion effect, labeled *direct engagement*, a *feeling* that occurs "when a user experiences direct interaction with the objects in a domain" [the notion of direct engagement is introduced in Laurel, 1986b]. Hutchins et al. add the requirements that input expressions be able to make use of previous output expressions, that the system create the illusion of instantaneous response (except where inappropriate to the domain), and that the interface be unobtrusive.

It seems likely that direct manipulation and direct engagement are head and tail of the same coin (or two handfuls of the same elephant)—one focusing on the qualities of action and the other focusing on subjective response. The basic issue

[3]The adjective *virtual* describes things—worlds, phenomena, etc.—that look and feel like reality but that lack the traditional physical substance. A virtual object, for instance, may be one that has no real-world equivalent, but the persuasiveness of its representation allows us to respond to it *as if* it were real.

is what is required to produce the feeling of taking action within a representational world, stripped of the "metacontext" of the interface as a discrete concern. Hutchins et al. sum it up this way: "Although we believe this feeling of direct engagement to be of critical importance, in fact, we know little about the actual requirements for producing it." Nevertheless, their analysis as well as Shneiderman's [1987] provide many valuable insights and useful examples of the phenomenon.

If we remove Shneiderman's clause regarding labeled button presses (because in many cases buttons are the artifacts of a pernicious interface metacontext), then the sense of directness can be boiled down to continuous representation, "physical" action, and apparent instantaneity of response. Apparent instantaneity depends upon both processing speed and the elimination of representations of intermediate activities in design. In the analyses of both Shneiderman and Hutchins et al., continuous representation and physical action depend heavily upon graphical representation. In fact, Hutchins et al. identify the granddaddy of direct manipulation as Ivan Sutherland's graphical design program, *Sketchpad* [Sutherland, 1963]. Graphical (and, by extension, multisensory) representations are fundamental to both the physical and emotional aspects of directness in interaction. Hence, it is worthwhile to examine the role and contributions of graphic design in the interface domain.

In many ways, the role of the graphic designer in human-computer interaction is parallel to the role of the theatrical scene designer. Both create representations of objects and environments that provide a context for action. In the case of theatre, the scene designer provides objects like teacups and chairs ("props"), canvas-covered wooden frames that are painted to look like walls ("flats"), and decorative things like draperies and rugs ("set dressing"). The behaviors of these elements is also designed—doors open, make-believe bombs explode, trick chairs break in barroom brawls. The lighting designer uses elements like color, intensity, and direction to illuminate the action and its environment and to focus our attention on key areas and events.

Both scene and light designers use such elements as line, shadow, color, texture, and style to suggest such contextual information as place, historical period, time of day, season, mood, and atmosphere. Theatrical designers also employ metaphor (and amplify the metaphors provided by the playwright) in the design of both realistic and nonrealistic pieces: the looming cityscape around Willy Loman's house in *Death of a Salesman* metaphorically represents his isolation and the death of his dreams; abstract webs of gauzy fabric suggest the multiple layers of illusion in the personality of Peer Gynt.

Likewise, in the world of interfaces, the graphic designer renders the objects and environments in which the action of the application or system will occur, imparting behaviors to some objects (like zoom-boxes and pop-up menus) and representing both concrete and ephemeral aspects of context through the use of such elements as line, shadow, color, intensity, texture, and style. Such familiar metaphors as desktops and windows provide behavioral and contextual cues about the nature of the activity that they support.

Both theatrical design and graphical interface design are aimed at creating representations of *worlds that are like reality only different*. But a scene design is not a whole play—for that we also need representations of character and action. Likewise, the element of graphical design is only part of the whole representation that we call an interface.

## Throw the Baggage Out

The previous section picks up some of the more promising threads in the evolving discipline of interface design. It also suggests that these elements alone may not be sufficient in defining the nature of human-computer interaction or in realizing it effectively, and it recommends theatre as an additional perspective. But it may not be productive for theatre people simply to join all the other cooks in the kitchen. I want to take the argument a step further and suggest that the concept of *interface* itself is a hopeless hash, and that we might do better to throw it out and begin afresh.

## A Definitional Digression

My frustration with the notion of the interface is as old as my involvement with computers. Perhaps the best way to explain it is to take a short excursion through the history of my personal view. I became involved with computers as a way to support myself while I was a graduate student in theatre. I thought that my career was going to take me to the stage, either as an actor or as a director. But a life in the theatre promised little in terms of income, and when a friend of mine started a little company to create computer software in 1977, I jumped at the chance to bolster my survival potential with some technical skills.

I became a software designer and programmer, working primarily on interactive fairy tales and educational programs for children. The company was called CyberVision, and the machine was a lowly 1802 processor with a four-color, low-resolution display and an alphanumeric keypad. The CyberVision computer was cassette-loaded with 2K of RAM, and it had the capacity to synchronize taped audio with animation on the screen. My first "feature" was an interactive, animated version of *Goldilocks*. Later, I created the first lip-synching on a microcomputer for a game of *Hangman* in which the evil executioner delivered menacing lines in a Transylvanian accent (all this with only sixteen lip positions). I immediately became immersed in translating my knowledge of drama and theatre to the task at hand because the two media were so obviously alike.

When CyberVision folded to its competition (an upstart company called Atari), I asked my boss to help me think about what kind of job to look for next. He said, "Why don't you go work for a bank? They need people to help design automated teller machines." "I don't know anything about *that*," I cried. "Of course you do," he replied. "That's human factors." In response to my blank look, he elaborated: "That's making computer things easy for people to use."

What a concept!

I ended up going to work for Atari, not for a bank, but the notion of ease of use as a design criterion fit neatly and permanently into my developing intuitions about how theatrical expertise could inform the art of designing software. There's nothing between the audience and the stage but some good illusion. Clearly, I was on the right track. But I hadn't run into the other "i" word yet.

After a few years in the software branch of the Atari home computer division, I decided to take time out to sit down and think through what I had come to believe about computers and theatre. (I also needed to begin my dissertation, which I had decided would be on that subject.) Alan Kay gave me the opportunity to do so in his research lab at Atari. "Interface" was every other word in the conversations of the bright young MIT wizards that populated the lab. I dimly perceived that there must be more to it than ease of use, and so signed up for a weekly seminar that one of the psychologists on the staff was conducting on the subject.

## *Models of the Interface*

The seminar began by looking at how the concept of interface was typically understood by people in the computer field. Figure 1.1 shows a schematic model of the interface. The shaded rectangle in the middle represents the interface, which encompasses what appears on the screen, hardware input/output devices, and their drivers.

Compelling as its simplicity might make it, this model was immediately dismissed by everyone in the group. In order for an interface to work, the person has to have some

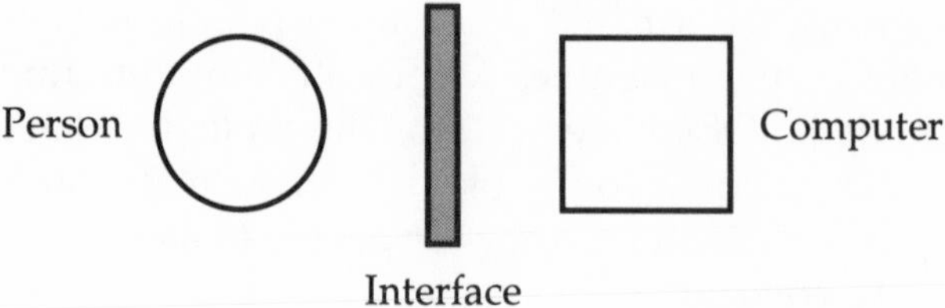


*Figure 1.1* **The pre-cognitive–science view of the interface.**

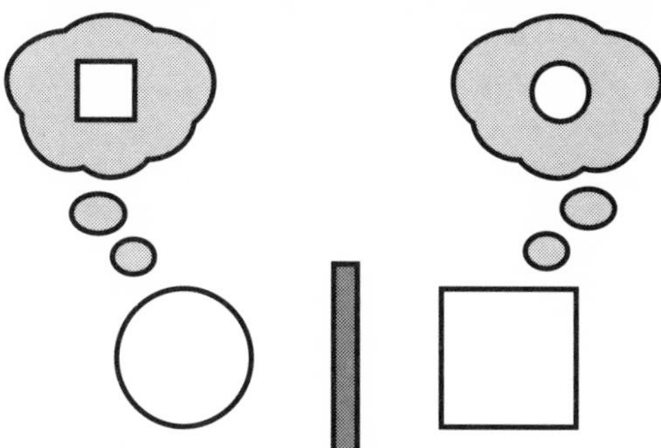

*Figure 1.2* **The mental-models view.** The thought bubbles and their contents are considered part of the interface.

idea about what the computer expects and can handle, and the computer has to incorporate some information about what the person's goals and behaviors are likely to be. These two phenomena—a person's "mental model" of the computer and the computer's "understanding" of the person—are just as much a part of the interface as its physical and sensory manifestations (Figure 1.2). However, in order to use an interface

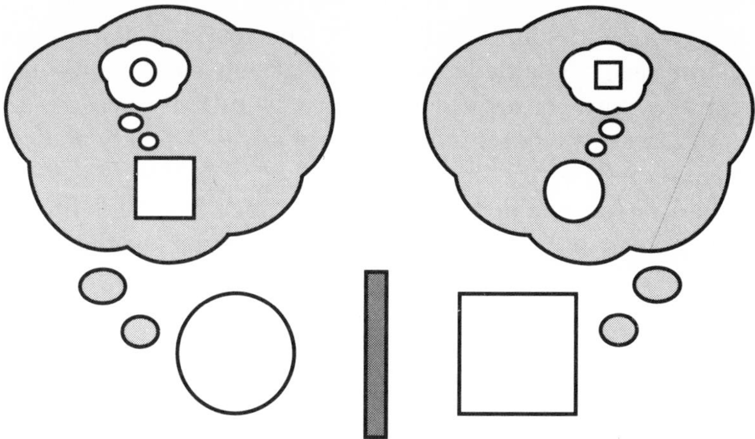

*Figure 1.3* **The "horrible recursion" version of the mental-models view of the interface.** More bubbles could be added ad infinitum.

*Figure 1.4* **A simple model of the interface, circa 1989.** In this view, the interface is that which joins human and computer, conforming to the needs of each.

correctly, you must also have an idea of what the computer is expecting you to do. If you are going to admit that what the two parties "think" about each other is part of what is going on, you will have to agree that what the two parties think about what the other is thinking about them must perforce be included in the model (Figure 1.3). This elaboration has dizzying ramifications.

Faced with this nightmare, our seminar at Atari abandoned the topic, and we turned our attention to more manageable concepts, such as the value of multisensory representations in the interface.

Over the years, I have frequently observed interface workers backing away from such gnarly theoretical discussions in favor of the investigation of more tractable issues of technique and technology—such subjects as direct manipulation, error handling, user testing, on-line help functions, graphics and animation, and sound and speech. The working definition of the interface has settled down to a relatively simple one—how humans and computers interact—but it avoids the central issue of what this all means in terms of reality and representation (Figure 1.4).

It occurs to me that when we have such trouble defining a concept, it usually means that we are barking up the wrong tree.

## *The World's a Stage*

For purposes of comparison, let's take a look at the theatre. We have observed that the theatre bears some similarities to interface design in that both deal with the representation of action. Drama, unlike novels or other forms of literature, incorporates the notion of *performance*; that is, plays are meant to be acted out. A parallel can be seen in interface design. In his book *The Elements of Friendly Software Design* [1982], Paul Heckel remarked, "When I design a product, I think of my program as giving a performance for its user." In the theatre, enactment typically occurs in a performance area called a stage (Figure 1.5). The stage is populated by one or more actors who portray characters. They perform actions in the physical context provided by the scene and light designers. The performance is typically viewed by a group of observers called an audience.

Part of the technical "magic" that supports the performance is embodied in the scenery and objects on the stage (windows that open and close; teacups that break); the rest happens in the backstage and "wing" areas (where scenery is supported, curtains are opened and closed, and sound effects are produced), the "loft" area above the stage, which accommodates lighting instruments and backdrops or set pieces that can be raised and lowered, and the lighting booth, which is usually above the audience at the back of the auditorium. The magic is created by both people and machines, but who, what, and where they are *do not matter* to the audience.

It's not just that the technical underpinnings of theatrical performance are unimportant to audience members; when a play is "working," audience members are simply not aware of the technical aspects at all. For the audience member who is

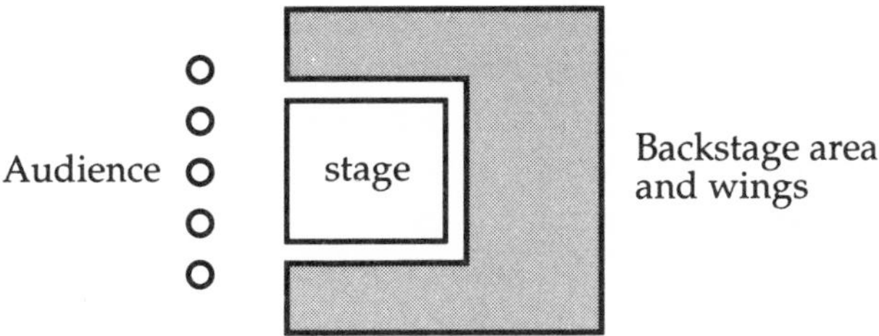


*Figure 1.5* **Plan view of a typical proscenium theatre.**

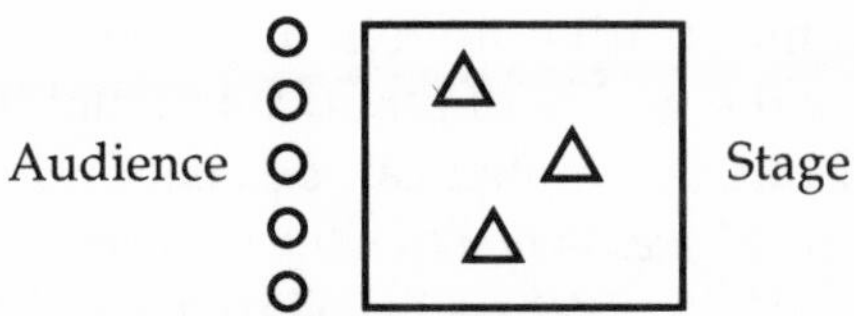


*Figure 1.6* For the audience, what's happening on the stage is all there is. The triangles represent the actors.

engaged by and involved in the play, the action on the stage is *all there is* (Figure 1.6). In this sense, plays are like movies: When you are engrossed in one, you forget about the projector, and you may even lose awareness of your own body. For the actor on stage, the experience is similar in that everything extraneous to the ongoing action is tuned out, with the exception of the audience's audible and visible responses, which are often used by the actors to tweak their performance in real time (this, by the way, reminds us that theatrical audiences are not strictly "passive" and may be said to influence the action). For actor and audience alike, the ultimate "reality" is what is happening in the imaginary world on the stage—the representation.

As researchers grapple with the notion of interaction in the world of computing, they sometimes compare computer users to theatrical audiences. "Users," the argument goes, are like audience members who are able to have a greater influence on the unfolding action than simply the fine-tuning provided by conventional audience response. In fact, I used this analogy in my dissertation in an attempt to create a model for interactive fantasy. The users of such a system, I argued, are like audience members who can march up onto the stage and become various characters, altering the action by what they say and do in their roles.

Let's reconsider for a minute. What would it be really like if the audience marched up on the stage? They wouldn't know the script, for starters, and there would be a lot of awkward fumbling for context. Their clothes and skin would look

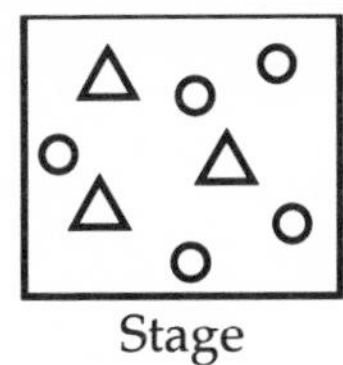


*Figure 1.7* Putting the audience on the stage creates confusion.

funny under the lights. A state of panic would seize the actors as they attempted to improvise action that could incorporate the interlopers and still yield something that had any dramatic integrity. Or perhaps it would degenerate into a free-for-all, as performances of avant-garde interactive plays in the 1960s often did (Figure 1.7).

The problem with the audience-as-active-participant idea is that it adds to the clutter, both psychological and physical. The transformation needs to be subtractive rather than additive. People who are participating in the representation aren't audience members anymore. It's not that the audience joins the actors on the stage; it's that they *become* actors—and the notion of "passive" observers disappears.

In a theatrical view of human-computer activity, the stage is a virtual world. It is populated by agents, both human and computer-generated, and other elements of the representational context (windows, teacups, desktops, or what-have-you). The technical magic that supports the representation, as in the theatre, is behind the scenes. Whether the magic is created by hardware, software, or wetware is of no consequence; its only value is in what it produces on the "stage." In other words, *the representation is all there is* (Figure 1.8). Think of it as existential WYSIWYG.[4]

---

[4]WYSIWYG stands for "what you see is what you get," coined by Warren Teitelman at Xerox PARC. It has been held up as a paradigm for direct-manipulation interfaces, but some theorists have contested its value (see, for instance, Ted Nelson's article, "The Right Way to Think About Software Design" in *The Art of Human-Computer Interface Design*.

*Figure 1.8* **An alternate view of human-computer interaction, in which the representation is all there is.** The triangles represent agents of either human or computer-generated types, and the other shapes are other objects in the virtual environment. The shape of the "stage" is oval, like the beam of a spotlight, to suggest that all that matters is that which is "illuminated."

## *Theatre as an Interface Metaphor*

The idea of human-computer activity suggests a number of interesting corollaries. Since all action is confined to the world of the representation, all agents are situated in the same context, have access to the same objects, and speak the same language. Participants learn what language to speak by noticing what is understood; they learn what objects are and what they do by playing around with them. A good example of this approach is a system called *Programming by Rehearsal*, developed by Laura Gould and William Finzer at Xerox PARC in 1983 and 1984. The system is a visual programming environment based on a dramatic metaphor. There are some problems with the application of the metaphor per se,[5] but the principle

[5]Particularly troublesome is the idea of combining a group of performers and a "smart" stage into another performer. This is a case where a novel capability stretches the metaphor to its breaking point. This particular example effectively blurs the distinction between stage and performer and alerts us to the fact that the terms are being used "only" metaphorically.

of "the representation is all there is" is applied consistently with powerful results:

> Two significant obstacles to learning a programming language are mastering the language's syntax and learning the vocabulary. In the Rehearsal World, the designers rarely have to know either the syntax or the vocabulary as most writing of code is done by watching. [Finzer and Fitzer, 1984]

A more recent attempt to employ a theatrical metaphor for an authoring system is Ellis Horowitz's SCriptWriter system, developed at the University of Southern California in 1987 and 1988 [Horowitz, 1988]. Horowitz's system further illustrates the distinction between using theatre as an interface metaphor and using it in the deeper way that this book advocates—as a fundamental understanding of what is going on in human-computer interaction.

As a metaphor, Horowitz's system successfully employs notions like "director" (as the code of a program generated by his system) and "rehearsal" (in the same way that Gould's system employs the notion of programming by rehearsal). But Horowitz's interface falls off the edge of its own metaphor in several ways. Programming actions like "cast" and "rehearse" are intermixed with traditional computerese terms like "edit," "list," and "print," failing on the level of consistency. The most disturbing inconsistency is the notion of treating a screen as a "player." His player concatenates the notions of stage, scenery, actors, and dialogue in a concept where the locus of agency is so dispersed as to be invisible. Furthermore, the notion of *human* agency—the other kind of "player" that may act upon a "stage"—is absent in Horowitz's conceptualization. The system does not support a notion of action that integrates human agency into the whole but rather leaves this aspect of design entirely up to the author.

## *Interactivity and Human Action*

The idea of enabling humans to take action in representational worlds is the powerful component of the programming-by-rehearsal approach. It is also what is missing in most attempts to use theatre simply as an interface metaphor. A central goal of this book is to suggest ways in which we can use a notion of theatre, not simply as a metaphor but as a way to conceptualize human-computer interaction itself.

Focusing on human agency allows us to simplify another consistently troublesome concept, the notion of "interactivity." People in the computer game business have been arguing about it for over a decade. In 1988, Alexander Associates sponsored INtertainment, the first annual conference bringing together people from all corners of the interactive entertainment business. People came from such diverse industries as personal computers, video games, broadcast and cable television, optical media, museums, and amusement parks. Over the course of the two days, a debate about the meaning of the word "interactive" raged through every session, disrupting carefully planned panels and presentations. People seemed to regard "interactivity" as the unique cultural discovery of the electronic age, and they demanded a coherent definition. Several speakers tried to oblige, but no one succeeded in presenting a definition that achieved general acceptance. Many participants departed angry and dissatisfied. Could it be the "wrong tree" problem again?

In the past, I've barked up that same tree. I posited that interactivity exists on a continuum that could be characterized by three variables: frequency (how often you could interact), range (how many choices were available), and significance (how much the choices really affected matters) [Laurel, 1986a and b]. A not-so-interactive computer game judged by these standards would let you do something only once in a while, would give you only a few things to choose from, and the things you could choose wouldn't make much difference to the whole action. A very interactive computer game (or desktop or flight simulator) would let you do something that really mattered at any time, and it could be anything you could think of—just like real life.

Now I believe that these variables provide only part of the picture. There is another, more rudimentary measure of interactivity: You either feel yourself to be participating in the ongoing action of the representation or you don't. Successful orchestration of the variables of frequency, range, and significance can help to create this feeling, but it can also arise from other sources—for instance, sensory immersion and the tight coupling of kinesthetic input and visual response. If a representation of the surface of the moon lets you walk around and look at things, then it probably feels extremely interactive, whether your virtual excursion has any consequences or not. It enables you to *act within a representation* that is important. Optimizing frequency and range and significance in human choice-making will remain inadequate as long as we conceive of the human as sitting on the other side of some barrier, poking at the representation with a joystick or a mouse or a virtual hand. You can demonstrate Zeno's paradox on the user's side of the barrier until you're blue in the face, but it's only when you traverse it that things get real.[6]

The experience of interactivity is a thresholdy phenomenon, and it is also highly context-dependent. The search for a definition of interactivity diverts our attention from the real issue: How can people participate as agents within representational contexts? Actors know a lot about that, and so do children playing make-believe. Buried within us in our deepest playful instincts, and surrounding us in the cultural conventions of theatre, film, and narrative, are the most profound and intimate sources of knowledge about interactive representations. A central task is to bring those resources to the fore and to begin to use them in the design of interactive systems.

So now we have at least two reasons to consider theatre as a promising foundation for thinking about and designing human-computer experiences. First, there is significant overlap in the fundamental objective of the two domains—that is, representing action with multiple agents. Second, theatre suggests the basis for a model of human-computer activity that is familiar, comprehensible, and evocative. The rest of this book

[6]Zeno's paradox (called the theory of limits in mathematics) says that you can never get from here to there because you can only get halfway, then halfway of halfway, etc. Mathematics offers a solution; so does common sense. But the paradox is compelling enough to have interested logicians and mathematicians for centuries.

will explore some of the theoretical and practical aspects of theatre that can be directly applied to the task of designing human-computer experiences. But there are a few more stones to be turned in arranging the groundwork for this discussion.

## *Is Drama Serious Enough?*

Because theatre is a form of entertainment, many people see it as fundamentally "non-serious." I have found that computer-science–oriented developers exhibit a high resistance to a theatrical approach to designing human-computer activity on the grounds that it somehow trivializes "serious" applications. Graphic designers undoubtedly have had to wrestle with the same sort of bias, design being seen not as a task of representation but one of mere decoration. Decoration is suspect because it may get in the way of the serious work to be done. (The same argument was used a few decades ago to ban bright colors, potted plants, and chatchkas from the workplace—but that's another story.) The fact of the matter is that graphics is an indispensable part of the representation itself, as amply demonstrated by the Macintosh and other contemporary computing environments.

The no-frills view that permeates thinking about the interfaces of "serious" applications is the result of a fundamental misunderstanding of the nature of seriousness in representations. The idea that theatre is "really not real" and is therefore unsuited as an approach to serious human-computer activities is misguided, because those activities are "really not real" in precisely the same ways. Without the representation, there is nothing at all—and theatre gives good representation.

Human-computer activity may be divided into two broad categories: productive and experiential [Laurel, 1986b]. Experiential activities, such as computer games, are undertaken purely for the experience afforded by the activity as you engage in it, while productive activities such as word processing have outcomes in the real world that are somehow beyond the experience of the activity itself. They are often mistakenly defined in terms of their artifacts—a printed document or a spreadsheet filled with numbers. But seriousness is not equivalent to concreteness. A printed paper (such as a page in this book, for example) has "real" implications (for example, transmitting knowledge, changing how something is done, receiving a grade, or getting paid) even though it is *itself* a representation. "Productivity" as a class of applications is better characterized not by the concreteness of outcomes but by their seriousness vis-a-vis the real world.

There is a parallel here with seriousness as an aspect of drama. In formal terms, "serious" treatments of subjects are reserved for tragedy (and in some senses, melodrama) and "non-serious" treatments are found in melodrama, comedy, farce, and satire. Here again, although the plays themselves are representations, seriousness depends largely on the consequences of the actions represented in them. In a serious work—in *Hamlet* for instance—falling down (as Ophelia does after her father's death) has serious consequences both physically and symbolically; in a farce, falling down (tripping over a piece of furniture or slipping on a banana peel, for instance) causes no permanent injury or pain to the agent.

To trace these effects through to the real world, we need to look at their impact on audiences. Ophelia's fall and its symbolic meaning impart information about suffering, revenge, and the consequences of evil that can be contemplated, absorbed, and acted upon by an audience. The fall of a clown, on the other hand, may arouse laughter and ephemeral pleasure; it may also, as in more thoughtful flavors of comedy, communicate a philosophical view (for example, a lighthearted attitude toward random accidents). Seriousness in both theatre and human-computer activities is a function of the subject and its treatment in both formal and stylistic terms. Drama provides means for representing the whole spectrum of activity, from the ridiculous to the sublime.

Another objection to a theatrical approach is that theatre by its very nature is "fuzzy," while serious applications of computers require crystal clarity. The connotation of fuzziness probably derives from drama's emphasis on emotion—

subjective experience—while serious productivity is seen to require undiluted objectivity. Yet such "serious" tasks as formatting a paper for publication or designing a business plan for a new product can involve a far greater degree of subjectivity (in terms of creativity and evaluation, for instance) than "objective" skill and action (cutting and pasting, typing, and mousing around). At the farthest extreme, the notion that serious applications require objectivity, clarity, and precision is used as a rationale for rejecting natural-language interaction. This is because the success of machine understanding, at least in leading contemporary approaches, is probabilistic, whereas the understanding of symbolic logic (in mathematical or numerical representations) is seen to be unambiguous.

Yet people often drown in precision because of the complexity and artificiality of its expression (both lexical and syntactic). From the adventure-gamer grappling with a parser to the inexperienced UNIX user trying to "alias" a complicated e-mail address, people experience the requirement for precision as troublesome. This is no secret; the problem is commonly acknowledged and wrestled with by most interface designers [for example, see Rubinstein and Hersh, 1984, Chapter 6]. What may stop them from making a foray into the world of dramatic representation is the view that drama is fundamentally imprecise and therefore prone to error (both in terms of interpretation and subsequent action), while people require 100 percent success in all of their communications with computers. My experience suggests that, in the vast majority of contexts, this simply isn't true.

The imprecision of dramatic representation is the price people pay—often quite enthusiastically—in order to gain a kind of lifelikeness, including the possibility of surprise and delight. When "imprecision" works, it delivers a degree of success that is, in balance against the effort required to achieve it, an order of magnitude more rewarding than the precision of programming, at least for the nonprogrammer. When it doesn't work (as in the case of a parser error), how it is experienced depends heavily upon how the system handles the failure. `"I DON'T UNDERSTAND THAT WORD"` disrupts and frustrates; an in-context response based on the most probable interpretation imitates a normal conversational failure and opens the way to methods of repair that are quite natural to use [see Brennan 1990b].

Both the frequency and robustness of the system's successes figure into the calculation of its value. A system that achieves only a moderate success rate (and no catastrophic failures) may be enthusiastically received if the successes are big ones, the effort required is minimal, and the overall experience is engaging. Chris Schmandt of the MIT Media Lab has developed a system that provides an extreme example. *Grunt* provides instructions for reaching a destination to the driver of a car. The system delivers directions via synthesized speech over a telephone. It listens to the driver for questions and cues about how well the driver has understood what it says. The trick is that the system is only listening to utterance pitch and duration and the duration of pauses—it *doesn't understand a single word.* Despite its low success rate (about 20 percent), *Grunt* has been received positively by most of its test users [see Schmandt, 1987 and 1990]. This is especially interesting in light of the fact that driving is viewed by most as a fairly serious activity, with strong real-world repercussions.

Seriousness in human-computer activities is a thresholdy thing. "Serious" and "non-serious" or "playful" activities can occur within the same context and at different stages in the same basic activity. I fool around with the layout of a document, for instance, experimenting with different fonts and paragraph styles, the placement of illustrations, perhaps even the structural divisions of the paper. At the point at which I make a creative decision and wish to implement a certain aspect of the design, I experience a "mode swing" (like a "mood swing," only different) toward greater "seriousness." I may then swing back to a "fooling around" mode as I evaluate the effects of a choice on the evolving document. In *Guides,* a research project at Apple investigating interfaces to multimedia databases, user testing revealed that people tend to move back and forth between browsing and focused searching "modes." They look around, then follow a line of investigation in an orderly and goal-directed fashion for a while, then begin to browse again. Apple researchers recorded similar behavior in the use of information kiosks that they installed at CHI '89 [Salomon, 1989]. Most of us have had similar experiences with encyclopedias, magazines, or even dictionaries.

The *Guides* project at Apple demonstrates this point. *Guides* was an investigation into the design and use of interface agents—computational characters that assist and interact with people. Most people who used the prototype *Guides* system were quite pleased to have the suggestions of the various guide characters about possible next moves in the database and to hear first-person stories that revealed a point of view about the content. They saw the guides as a great enhancement to the experience of browsing. At the same time, many saw the guides as impediments to goal-directed searching; that is, when they knew what they were looking for, the guides seemed to get in the way. There was simply too much indirection. One had to hope that the guide was "smart" enough to figure out what was sought and not to overlook anything relevant, and there was no way to find out for sure how well the guide was doing. There was also no way to chunk the guides' stories or to search through them with efficiency or acuity for smaller pieces of information. The *Guides* researchers were tempted to view these results as a need for a clearer, more "objective" approach to goal-directed searching.

In fact, that was only part of what people wanted. Many expressed the desire to be able to say to a guide, "go find this and only this and don't bother telling me how you feel about it," but there was no way to have such a conversation. The problem arose precisely at the threshold of "seriousness" that is crossed when shifting from an *experiential* mode (browsing) to an *instrumental* mode (goal-directed searching). There are two basic approaches to a solution. The first is to shift the locus of control from delegation to direct human agency. This approach would replace the guides with a representational environment containing the means for people to search the database themselves by topic or keyword. It corresponds roughly to the concept of a library, where you can move around among shelves of books that are arranged topically, occasionally picking one up and leafing through it. Of course, the virtual library is augmented by representational magic—books open to a page indicated by spoken keywords, stairs need not be climbed, and there is always enough light.

The second approach is to create a kind of agent that is capable of understanding a person's goal and delivering a successful result smoothly and efficiently—a kind of augmented reference librarian. Such an agent could theoretically deliver a bigger win in a couple of ways. First, it could preserve continuity in the representational context by continuing to employ agents. Second, it could still shift the locus of control to the person by making the searching agent more explicitly subservient and responsive. Third, it creates the possibility for results beyond those that could be achieved by a person examining the database in the first person—no matter how magical the virtual library might be, searching it thoroughly would quickly exceed the human thresholds for both tedium and complexity. For instance, a searching agent might not only look at the topical index but also access topical data that might be associated with smaller chunks of information—data that would be too numerous for a person to examine in detail. A searching agent might then provide an array of possible information sources as the result of its search, each cued up to the most relevant chunk. Here the potential for surprise and delight is optimized, making the experience more pleasurable. Such powers of agents will be discussed in greater detail in the section on agents in Chapter 5.

In summary, a dramatic approach need not be fuzzy or imprecise in its ability to produce results. It is potentially capable of supporting both serious and nonserious activities. Its evocative powers and even its ambiguities can be harnessed to enhance rather than to impede a person's serious goals, and to create the possibility of surprise and delight—things that are rarely produced by exhaustive responses to crystal-clear specifications.

For many people whose way of working can be characterized as objective or scientific, the idea of employing an artistic approach is troublesome. It's hard to say how artists do what they do. The process seems to consist largely of imagination and inspiration, and there seems to be no forthright, dependable methodology. Yet, as we observed in the Foreword, and as we will expand upon in the next chapter, there are ways in which art is "lawful"; that is, there are formal, structural, and causal dimensions that can be identified and used both descriptively and productively. The final goal of this chapter is to justify taking an *artistic* approach to the problem of designing human-computer activity.

## An Artistic Perspective

In his seminal book, *The Elements of Friendly Software Design* [1982], Paul Heckel characterizes software design as primarily concerned with communication. He observes that "among all the art forms that can teach us about communication, the most appropriate is filmmaking." Heckel chooses filmmaking as an example over older forms (such as theatre) because it "illustrates the transition from an engineering discipline to an art form." He goes on to observe that movies did not achieve wide popular success until artists replaced engineers as the primary creators. Heckel's book is filled with references to illusion, performance, and other theatrical and filmic metaphors with software examples to illustrate each observation. He gives the use of metaphor in interface design a different twist by employing filmmaking, writing, acting, and other "communication crafts" as metaphors for the process of software design.

In 1967, Ted Nelson examined the evolution of film in order to understand how the new medium he envisioned—hypertext—should develop. In considering the ways in which the stage had influenced film, he noted that "stage content, when adapted, was appropriate and useful, while stage techniques (such as the notion of a proscenium and an insistence on continuous action within scenes) were not [Nelson in Schecter, 1967]. From the vantage point of 1990, we can see a migration of both techniques and content from film into the computer medium. If one takes the theatre and the film medium as subsets of a larger category, as representations of action in virtual worlds, then another key similarity between these media and computers is their fundamental elements of form and structure and their purpose.

Both Heckel and Nelson draw our attention to the centrality of "make-believe" in the conception and design of software. An engineer's view of software design is rooted in logic, realizing an orderly set of functions in an internally elegant program. In Heckel's view, the better approach is rooted in vision, which realizes an environment for action through evocative, consistent illusions. According to Nelson, it is the creation of "virtualities"—representations for things that may never have existed in the real world before [Nelson, 1990]. The role of imagination in creating interactive representations is clear and cannot be overrated. In an important sense, a piece of computer software is a collaborative exercise of the imaginations of the creator(s) of a program and people who use it.

Imagination supports a constellation of distinctively human phenomena that includes both symbolic thinking and representation-making. There is a story about a monkey and some bananas that every undergraduate psychology student has heard. A researcher places a monkey in a room with a bunch of bananas hanging from the ceiling and a box on the floor. The monkey tries various ways of getting the bananas—reaching, jumping, and so on—and eventually climbs up onto the box. A person in a similar situation would rehearse most of the possible strategies in her head and actively pursue only those that seemed promising, maybe only the successful one. For the monkey, the focus of attention is the real bananas; for the human, it's what's going on inside her head. Imagination is a shortcut through the process of trial and error.

But imagination is good for much more than real-world problem solving. The impulse to create interactive representations, as exemplified by human-computer activities, is only the most recent manifestation of the age-old desire to make what we imagine palpable—our insatiable need to exercise our intellect, judgment, and spirit in contexts, situations, and even personae that are different from those of our everyday lives. When a person considers how to climb a tree, imagination serves as a laboratory for virtual experiments in physics, biomechanics, and physiology. In matters of justice, art, or philosophy, imagination is the laboratory of the spirit.

What we do in our heads can be merely expedient or far-reaching, private or intended for sharing and communication. The novels of Ayn Rand, for instance or the plays of George Bernard Shaw create worlds where people address issues and problems, both concrete and abstract, and enact their discoveries, responses, and solutions. These representations are wholly contained in the realm of the imagination, yet they transport us to alternate possible perspectives and may influence us in ways that are more resonant and meaningful than experiences actually lived.

Art is the external *representation* of things that happen in the head of the artist. Art forms differ in terms of the materials they employ, the way the representations are created, what they purport to represent, and how they are manifest in the world. Different forms have different powers—the powers to engage, to provide pleasure and information, to evoke response. But all have as their end the *representation* of some internal vista that the artist wishes to create beyond the bounds of his or her own skull, making it available in some form to other people.

What are such representations good for? Aristotle defined *catharsis* as the end cause of a play and saw it as the pleasurable release of emotion, specifically those emotions evoked by the action represented in the play.[7] In his view, catharsis occurred during the actual "run-time" of the play, but some contemporary theorists disagree. The early twentieth-century

---

[7]That's not to say that plays must arouse only pleasant emotions; the pleasure of release makes even nasty emotions enjoyable in a theatrical context. Catharsis is discussed more fully in Chapter 4.

German dramatist Bertolt Brecht extended the notion of catharsis beyond the temporal boundary of the performance [Brecht, 1964]. He posited that catharsis is not complete until the audience members take what they have assimilated from the representation and put it to work in their lives. In Brecht's hypothesis, the representation lives between imagination and reality, serving as a conductor, amplifier, clarifier, and motivator.

It seems to me that computer-based representations work in fundamentally the same way: a person participates in a representation that is not the same as real life but which has real-world effects or consequences. Representation and reality stand in a particular and necessary relation to one another. In much contemporary thinking about interfaces, however, the understanding of that relationship is muddy. On the one hand, we speak of "tools" for "users" to employ in the accomplishment of various tasks with computers. We plumb psychology for information about how people go about using tools and what is the best way to design them. We arrive at notions like "cut" and "paste" and even "write" that seem to suggest that people working with computers are operating in the arena of the concrete. We often fail to see that these are *representations* of tools and activities and to notice how that makes them different from (and often better than) the real thing.

On the other hand, we employ graphic artists to create icons and windows, pictures of little hands and file folders and lassos and spilling paint cans, to stand in for us in the computer's world. Here the idea of representation is used, but only in a superficial sense. Messy notions like "interface metaphor" are employed to gloss over the differences between representation and reality, attempting to draw little cognitive lines from the things we see on the screen to the "real" activities that psychologists tell us we are performing. Interface metaphors rumble along like Rube Goldberg machines, patched and wired together every time they break, until they are so encrusted with the artifacts of repair that we can no longer interpret them or recognize their referents.

This confusion over the nature of human-computer activity can be alleviated by thinking about it in terms of theatre, where the special relationship between representation and reality is already comfortably established, not only in theoretical terms but also in the way that people design and experience theatrical works. Both domains employ representations as contexts for thought. Both attempt to amplify and orchestrate experience. Both have the capacity to represent actions and situations that do not and cannot exist in the real world, in ways that invite us to extend our minds, feelings, and senses to envelop them.

In the view of semioticist Julian Hilton [1991], theatre is "essentially the art of showing, the art of the index . . . . It involves the synthesis of symbolic and iconic systems (words and moving pictures) in a single indivisible performed event." Hilton employs the myth of Pygmalion and Galathea (familiar to many as the basis of George Bernard Shaw's *Pygmalion* and its musical adaptation, *My Fair Lady*) to express the relationship of the theatre to the domain of artificial intelligence. He describes the value of the theatre's ability to represent things that have no real-world referents in semiotic terms:

> Galathea in a literal sense imitates nothing, and as such defines a class of icon (the statue after all is a picture of itself) that can simultaneously be an index. It is this category of non-imitative index which enables the index to liberate its true power, whereby it has all the infinite valency of the symbol while retaining the immediate recognisability of the icon. [Hilton, 1991]

Computers are representation machines that can emulate any known medium, as Alan Kay observes:

> The protean nature of the computer is such that it can act like a machine or like a language to be shaped and exploited. It is a medium that can dynamically simulate the details of any other medium, including media that cannot exist physically. It is not a tool, although it can act like many tools. It is the first metamedium, and as such it has degrees of freedom for representation and expression never before encountered and as yet barely investigated. [Kay, 1984]

Thinking about interfaces is thinking too small. Designing human-computer experience isn't about building a better desktop. It's about creating imaginary worlds that have a special relationship to reality—worlds in which we can extend, amplify, and enrich our own capacities to think, feel, and act. Hopefully, this chapter has persuaded you that knowledge from the theatrical domain can help us in that task. The next two chapters are designed to give you a deeper understanding of some of the most relevant aspects of dramatic theory and to apply them to interactive forms.

Chapter Two

# *Dramatic Foundations, Part I: Elements of Qualitative Structure*

## *Delayed Gratification*

The purpose of this chapter and the next is to provide a framework of dramatic theory that can be applied to the task of designing human-computer experiences. Such experiences are structured around the fundamental precepts of dramatic form and structure and are based primarily on Aristotelian poetics—poetics being a term used to describe a body of theory that treats a poetic or aesthetic domain. We will take up each basic idea and then adapt it to the human-computer context, arriving at what may be described as a *poetics of interactive form* (remember that we defined "interactivity" to mean the ability of humans to participate in actions in a representational context). Once we have constructed a theoretical base, we can then go on to explore its implications in some selected areas of design.

This approach necessitates that you endure some delayed gratification. You will be forced to wade through a welter of analogies, definitions, and hypotheses before a coherent picture can emerge. Hopefully, the case presented in the first chapter is sufficiently persuasive to lure you into taking the journey. By the end of the next chapter we will be able to pull the various elements together into a useful theory.

## Hoary Poetics

People often find it quite peculiar that I turn to a theory that is over two thousand years old to gain insight into a very recent phenomenon. Even those who can be persuaded that artistic and literary theories may be useful in the computer domain have difficulty with what they perceive as an extremely antiquated approach. Why Aristotle? How can it be useful to us today to employ concepts that were defined in the fourth century B.C.? Aren't there more contemporary views that would be more appropriate to the task?

I want to answer the latter question first. Without a doubt there are more recent theorists who have made major contributions to the body of dramatic criticism; the next few chapters will touch on the work of many of them. But no one has provided a theory of the drama that is as comprehensive and well-integrated as Aristotle's; no one has needed to. For most, the *Poetics* has been a jumping-off place—a body of ideas to tweak and elaborate on. For some, it has been something to bounce off of; many theorists (such as Bertolt Brecht, as mentioned in Chapter 1) have persuasively amended Aristotle's poetics on certain points. But no one has presented a fully formulated alternative view of the nature of the drama that has achieved comparably wide acceptance.

A second reason for looking to the *Poetics* as opposed to more contemporary theories (such as post-structuralism) is that the Aristotelian paradigm is more appropriate to the state of the technology to which we are trying to apply it. In order to build representations that have theatrical qualities in computer-based environments, a deep, robust, and logically coherent notion of structural elements and dynamics is required—and this is what Aristotle provides.

Aristotle (384–322 B.C.) was a student and successor of the philosopher Plato. His many works (including *Ethics*,

*Rhetoric*, *Physics*, and *Metaphysics*) encompassed what we would today call both philosophical and scientific thought, exploring subjects from biology to logic, government to art. He was tutor to Alexander the Great, whose assumption of power in 336 B.C. ushered in the Hellenistic Age.

Aristotle worked and wrote in the century after the great blossoming of Greek drama, exemplified by the works of Aeschylus (525–456 B.C.), Sophocles (496–406 B.C.), Euripides (484–406/7 B.C.), and Aristophanes (448–380 B.C.). During the brightening days of the fifth century B.C., theatre seemed to spring full-blown from the brows of these early dramatists.

Looking back on that remarkable century, Aristotle set himself the task of understanding where the various forms of poetry, including narrative, lyric, and dramatic, came from and how they work. Aristotle's work was a response to criticisms of poetry leveled by his teacher, Plato. Plato asserted that the poetic process is fundamentally incoherent and defies explanation; Aristotle described the process of poetic composition in logical terms. Plato complained that drama and poetry did not "inculcate virtue"; Aristotle countered by describing and defending the value of the things that poetry does accomplish:

> [Poetry] aims at pleasure, but at the rational pleasure which is a part of the good life; by its representation of serious action it does indeed excite emotions, but only to purge them and so to leave the spectator strengthened; since art represents universals and not particulars, it is nearer to the truth than actual events and objects are, not further from it, as Plato maintained.
> [Kitto, 1967]

Aristotle is often referred to as the progenitor of western science because of the methods of observation and inquiry that he employed as well as his insatiable and wide-ranging curiosity. A common objection to his dramatic theory is that it is too prescriptive; the *Poetics* is mistakenly viewed as a book of rules. (This is due in large part to the neoclassical critics of the Renaissance, many of whom distorted Aristotle's work to support their belief that drama should provide explicit moral instruction.) The truth is that Aristotle's goal was to observe, analyze, and report on the nature of the drama, not to generate rules for producing it. His theories may be used productively, not because they are recipes but because they identify and elucidate drama's formal and structural characteristics.

## The Cultural Backdrop

The great Greek tragedies of the fifth and early fourth centuries B.C. were performed at the festivals of Dionysus, the Greek god of nature, wine, fertility, and celebration. Students of modern popular culture will recognize Dionysus (also known as Bacchus in Roman mythology) as the giddy wine-stained god astride the donkey in the "Pastoral" sequence of Walt Disney's *Fantasia*. Although revelry was certainly a major part of Dionysus' gestalt, he was a somewhat more imposing figure than the Disney representation suggests. The spirit he embodied was at the wellspring of life; his was the energy on which survival utterly depends.

The festivals of Dionysus were annual events that celebrated the symbolic death and rebirth of the god, and hence nature. Several plays were commissioned for performance at each festival and they competed for the prize awarded to the best drama. The theatrical people who were involved in the production of the plays (including actors, musicians, and costumers) maintained a strong connection to the Dionysian religion, eventually forming a guild whose head was usually a Dionysian priest.

Early Greek drama sprang from the intersection of philosophy, religion, and art. The occasion was ostensibly religious, and there is reason to believe that at least some of the actors felt themselves to be "in possession of the god" in whose festival they performed. The subjects chosen by the great tragic playwrights for theatrical representation at such festivals were matters of serious import, depicting the evolution of Greek philosophy through their dramatic treatment of known

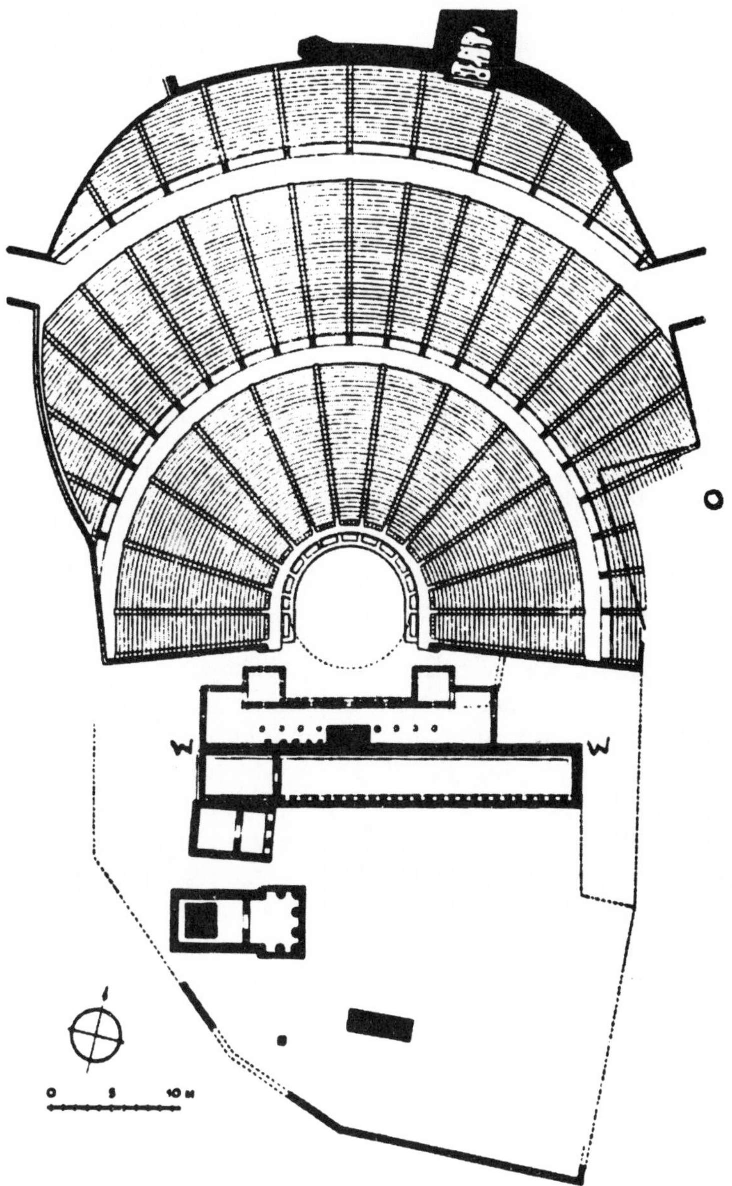


*Figure 2.1* **The Theatre of Dionysus in Athens.** It was at this site that most of the great Greek tragedies were originally performed.

Illustration taken from Dörpfeld and Reisch's *Das Griechische Theater* (Athens, 1896). Courtesy of the Jerome Lawrence and Robert E. Lee Theatre Research Institute, The Ohio State University.

myths and stories, such as the tragedies of Agamemnon, Orestes, and Oedipus. They communicated philosophical and religious ideas as well as providing the occasion for the collective experience of emotion. Quite simply, Greek drama was the way that Greek culture publicly thought and felt about the most important issues of humanity, including ethics, morality, government, and religion. To call drama merely "entertainment" in this context is to miss most of the picture. Imagine how our own culture would be transformed if the basic fare of television, for instance, were the same subjects as those treated by the Greek theatre. What if television were the way for our whole culture to consider matters of deepest import? The human need for such forums has not changed, but television seems to be the only pervasive means American society has devised for meeting it. A case can therefore be made that the trivial content and impoverished range of points of view that characterize commercial television diminish the human spirit by diminishing what we think about and how we think about it. The Greeks employed drama and theatre as *tools for thought*, in much the same way that we employ computers today—or at least in the ways that we envision employing them in the not-too-distant future.

In science as well as in art, the Greeks of the fifth and fourth centuries B.C. were discovering and inventing a world of unprecedented scope and order through the rapidly evolving tools of philosophy. In exploring the nature of the drama and other arts, Aristotle employed the same conception of causality to which he attributed the forms of living things, and that is a good place to begin.

## *The Four Causes, or Why Things Are the Way They Are*

How does a representation—a play or a human-computer activity—get to be the way it is? What defines its nature, its shape, its particulars? What forces are at work? If you are tempted to balk at this excursion into the deepest regions of theory, let me remind you of the reason for taking it: Understanding how things work is necessary if we are to know how to make them. When a made thing is flawed or unsuccessful, it may not be due to poor craftsmanship. Architects have designed and built beautiful buildings that wouldn't stand up; playwrights have written plays with mellifluous words and solid dramatic structure that closed after one night in New Jersey; and engineers have designed software with lovely screens and loads of "functionality" that leaves people pounding on their keyboards in frustration. The reason for failure is often a lack of understanding about how a thing works, what its nature is, and what it will try to be and do—whether you want it to or not—because of its intrinsic form.

The four causes are forces that operate concurrently and interactively during the process of creation. Although Aristotle also applied them to living organisms, our discussion will be restricted to the realm of made things. We will begin with definitions of the four causes and then apply them, first to drama, and then to human-computer activity.[1]

- *Formal cause:* The formal cause of a thing is the form or shape of what it is trying to be. For example, the formal cause of a building is the architect's notion of what its form will be when it is finished. Those formal properties of "building-ness" (or "church-ness," or "house-ness," etc.) that are independent of any particular instance of a building (or church or house) and which define what a building is are one component of the formal cause. They are filtered through the mind of the architect, where they are particularized by various design contingencies (there needs to be sunlight in the morning room; the conference room needs to accommodate a group of fifty, etc.), as well as his or her own values, tastes, and ideas.

[1] I have employed the traditional terminology, not out of a desire to promote philosophical jargon but because it is quite difficult to find synonyms that do these concepts justice, and also because more casual terminology can lead to confusion downstream.

Formal cause operates through an idea or vision of the completed whole, which will undergo change and elaboration as the process of creation unfolds; that is, there is a reciprocal relationship between the formal cause and the work in progress. The formal cause for a thing may be muddy or clear, constant or highly evolutionary, but it is always present.

- *Material cause:* The material cause of a thing is what it is made of. So, to pursue the architecture example, the material cause of a building includes stones or concrete or wood, glass, nails, mortar, and so on. Note that the properties of the materials influence the properties of the structure; for example, wood is more flexible than steel, but steel is stronger.
- *Efficient cause:* The efficient cause of a thing is the way in which it is actually made. This includes both the maker and the tools. For instance, two buildings with the same architectural plan and the same materials created by different builders with different skills and tools will differ in terms of their efficient cause.
- *End cause:* The end cause of a thing is its purpose—what it is intended to *do* in the world once it is completed. In architecture, a building is intended to accommodate people, living or working or playing or performing operas or whatever, according to the kind of building it is.

Now let's apply these four causes to the theatre:

- *Formal cause:* The completed plot—that is, the *whole action* that the playwright is trying to represent. The whole action subsumes notions of form and genre and the patterns that define them.
- *Material cause:* The stuff a play is made up of—the sounds and sights of the actors as they move about on the stage. Note that the material of a play is not words, as one might think from reading a script. That's because plays are intended to be acted out, and there's more to enactment than words. The *enactment* is the performance—that which unfolds before the eyes and ears of the audience.

- *Efficient cause:* The skills, tools, and techniques of the playwright, actors, and other artists who contribute to the finished play.
- *End cause:* The pleasurable arousal and expression of a particular set of emotions in the audience (*catharsis*).

As mentioned in the section on catharsis in Chapter 1, "pleasurable" is a key word in understanding catharsis; emotions aroused by plays are not experienced in the same way as emotions aroused by "real" events, and even the most negative emotions can be pleasurable in a dramatic context (the success of such film genres as suspense and horror depends on this fact). Various historical periods have added "riders" like political consciousness-raising or moral instruction to the end cause. It is safe to say that since emotion depends upon the successful communication of content, then some level of communication is implicit in the end cause. We will explore this aspect further in the discussion of causality and universality in Chapter 3.

## The Four Causes of Human-Computer Activity

How can we define these four causes for human-computer activities? In this discussion it is difficult to avoid using computer-related terminology, which is in many cases already loaded with connotations that are not always appropriate. Among these terms are *functionality, program, application, representation,* and *agent*.

In computerese, *functionality* refers to the things that a program does—a spreadsheet can make calculations of certain types, for instance, and a word processor can do such things as move text around, display different fonts, and check spelling. Interface designers often describe their task as representing a program's functionality [for example, see Rubinstein and Hersh, 1984, p. 19]. But this understanding of functionality brings us to the tree falling in the forest again. A spreadsheet's ability to crunch numbers in certain ways is only *potential* until a person gives it some numbers to crunch and tells it how to crunch them, in fine or gross detail. Thus the definition of functionality needs to be reconceived as *what a person can do with a program,* rather than what a program has the capacity to do. This definition lands us back in the territory of action with human and computer agents. It also contains a word we haven't used before: "program."

A program is a set of instructions that defines the potential actions that make up a human-computer activity and their representations. These actions and representations may change as a result of ongoing action (for instance, as the result of capturing or inferring people's preferences). A program also defines the environment for action and the other objects that inhabit that environment, including their representations and capabilities. Actually, the elements of action and environment and their representations are usually the result of more than one program—with the Macintosh, for instance, certain aspects of the "interface" are embedded in the operating system and Finder code. Of course, the potential of a program is also shaped by the hardware for which it is written—what kind of math it can perform, for instance, and the qualities of its graphical display.

In theatrical terms, a program (or a cluster of interacting programs) is analogous to a script, including its stage directions. A script is constrained by the physical realities of the kind of theatre in which it is to be performed and the capabilities of the stage machinery and actors. Program code is equivalent to the *words* of a script (including the theatre's own brand of jargon—for example, "move stage left" or "counter-cross"). In his investigations of artificial intelligence, Julian Hilton adds another dimension to this analogy:

> The text [of a play] therefore, is a combination of explicit and implicit notational systems which have as their initial purpose the enablement of an event in which performers and audience can share as partners. While obviously the notion of a computer was alien to Shakespeare, that of his theatre as a complex space-time machine was certainly not . . . . [Hilton, 1991]

Functionality is equivalent to the script parsed not by words but by *actions*. An apparent difference between programs and theatrical scripts is that programs are not intrinsically linear in form, while scripts generally are. At the highest level, this nonlinearity means that programs can cause different things to happen depending upon the actions of their users. The way in which computer functionality differs from dramatic action is that some portion of it is shaped by a person as the action unfolds; that is, "authorship" is collaborative in real time (this aspect will be further explored below in the discussion of plot). In summary, then, *functionality consists of the actions that are performed by people and computers working in concert, and programs are the means for creating the potential for those actions.*

An "application" is generally described as a program designed to deliver a particular functionality to "end-users," which is distinct from the type of programs that are not directly accessible to people, such as those which live deep in the bowels of missile silos and operating systems. Informal taxonomies of applications exist; for example, applications for word processing and spreadsheets belong to the larger class of productivity applications; drawing, painting, and music programs are often classified as "creativity" applications; and adventure, action, and strategy games are "entertainment" applications. *The most important way in which applications, like plays, are individuated from one another is by the particular actions that they represent.* Applications are analogous to individual plays; the larger categories are analogous to genres and forms of plays (tragic, comic, didactic, etc.).

We have used the word "representation" throughout Chapter 1 to distinguish the shadowy realms of art and human-computer activity from phenomenal reality. Webster's defines a representation as "an artistic likeness or image" (and also, incidentally, as "a dramatic production or performance"). The Greek word for artistic representation is *mimesis*. Both plays and human-computer activities are *mimetic* in nature; that is, they exhibit the characteristics of artistic representations. A mimesis is a made thing, not an accidental or arbitrary one: using a pebble to represent a man is not mimetic; making a doll to represent him is. We often use the word "representation" followed by "of" and then the name of some object—a character is a representation of a person, a landscape painting is a representation of a place. But in art as in human-computer activities, the object of a mimesis (i.e., that which it is intended to represent) may be a real thing or a virtual one; that is, a thing that exists nowhere other than the imagination. A play may be a mimesis of events (literally, a series of actions) that are taken from history or that are entirely "made up." *Mimetic representations do not necessarily have real-world referents.*

In computerese, two kinds of representations are acknowledged: internal and external representations. In the Macintosh Finder, for instance, a page icon is the external representation of a document. Both the document and the icon have internal representations that consist of the code that defines them—how they look and behave. However, in keeping with the principle that "the representation is all there is," an internal representation has no value by itself—just as the script for a performance is never seen (and hopefully never thought about) by an audience. As a program, an internal representation is merely the potential for what may be manifest in the external representation—that which has sensory and functional properties. As it is used in this book, the term "representation" subsumes both aspects.

We have said that human-computer activities can be defined as representations of actions with agents of both human and computer origin. The word "agents" has a particular meaning in computerese, which is a derivation of the more general sense of the word. A computer-based "agent" is defined as a bundle of functionality that performs some task for a person, either in real time or asynchronously. An example is the mail-sorting agents developed by Thomas Malone in the Object Lens project [Crowston and Malone, 1988]. Agents may be represented anthropomorphically —that is, as characters—but they need not be. The Aristotelian definition of an agent is the root of both of these permutations: *An agent is one who initiates and performs actions.* So in any human-computer activity, there is at least one agent—the human who turns on the machine—and if the machine does anything after it boots, then there are at least two. This book uses the more general definition because, as we will see later in this chapter, computer-based agency is present in all human-computer activities, whether or not it is coalesced into coherent agent-like "entities" in the representation.

Given these definitions, we can now take a run at the four causes as applied to human-computer activity:

- *Formal cause:* The formal cause of a particular human-computer activity is the form of what it is trying to be. Human-computer interaction generally lacks the kind of well-known formal categories offered by drama (comedy, tragedy, etc.).[2] What we can say, however, is that the *form* of human-computer activity is a representation of action with agents that may be either human, computer-based, or a combination of both. We will discover more of the characteristics of that form as we identify its structural elements and the relations among them.
- *Material cause:* The material cause of a human-computer activity, and also of a play, is the enactment—that which unfolds before a person's senses. As plays employ the sights and sounds produced by actors moving about in scenic environments, computers may employ graphics, sound and music, text characters, and even tactile and kinesthetic effects. In the discussion of structural elements below, we will see how these sensory materials are shaped into more sophisticated constructs.

---

[2] Although application categories like "word processing" or "productivity" are sometimes invoked by designers as if they were formal criteria, I would argue that they are rather part of the end cause, since their definitions are essentially functional rather than formal. As most computer-using writers know, it is still impossible to derive the "canonical" form of a word processor from all of the instances that exist on the market; we can speak only about a word processor's expected or necessary functionality.

- *Efficient cause:* The efficient cause of a human-computer activity is the skills and tools of its maker(s). Since a given application is probably based, at least in part, on chunks of program code that have been created by other people for other purposes, the computer equivalent of a playwright is usually a group of people. Both theatre and human-computer activity design are collaborative disciplines; both depend upon a variety of artistic and technical contributions. In both domains, the quality and nature of these contributions are strongly influenced by the available tools. Theatrical artists today are increasingly relying on computer-based tools for such tasks as lighting and scene design, lighting execution, moving scenery, designing costumes, storing and simulating dance notation and period movements, and, of course, writing scripts. Theatrical folk express the same frustrations with their tools as graphic designers and other artists who are working in the computer medium itself.

- *End cause:* The end cause of a human-computer activity is what it is intended to *do* in the world once it is completed. Thus the end cause obviously involves functionality: Word processors had better spit out documents. But experience is an equally important aspect of the end cause; that is, what a person thinks and feels about the activity is part of its reason for being the way it is. At the very least, a person must understand the activity well enough to do something. At best, he or she should be engaged, pleased, or even delighted by the experience. This aspect of the end cause seems trivial to many; it is too often handed off as an afterthought to harried interface designers who follow programmers around with virtual brooms and pails. How much better it is to place the notion of pleasurable experience where it can achieve the best results—as part of the necessary nature of human-computer activity.

## The Six Elements and Causal Relations Among Them

One of Aristotle's fundamental ideas about drama (as well as other forms of literature) is that a finished play is an *organic whole*. He used the term *organic* to evoke an analogy with living things. Insofar as a whole organism is more than the sum of its parts, all of the parts are necessary for life, and the parts have certain necessary relationships to one another. He identified six qualitative elements of drama and suggested the relationships among them in terms of formal and material causality.[3]

I present Aristotle's model here for two reasons. First, I am continually amazed by the elegance and robustness of the categories and their causal relations. Following the causal relations through as one creates or analyzes a drama seems to automagically reveal the ways in which things should work or exactly how they have gone awry. Second, Aristotle's model creates a disciplined way of thinking about the design of a play in both constructing and debugging activities. Because of its fundamental similarities to drama, human-computer activity can be described with a similar model, with equal utility in both design and analysis.

Table 2.1 lists the elements of qualitative structure in hierarchical order. Here is the trick to understanding the hierarchy: Each element is the formal cause of all those below it, and each element is the material cause of all those above it. As you move up the list of elements from the bottom, you can see how each level is a successive refinement—a *shaping* —of the materials offered by the previous level. The following sections expand upon the definitions of each of the elements in ascending order.

---

[3]The explicit notion of the workings of formal and material causality in the hierarchy of structural elements is, although not apocryphal, certainly neo-Aristotelian. See Smiley [1971].

| Element | In Drama | In Human-Computer Activity |
|---|---|---|
| **Action** | The whole action being represented. The action is theoretically the same in every performance. | The whole action, as it is collaboratively shaped by system and user. The action may vary in each interactive session. |
| **Character** | Bundles of predispositions and traits, inferred from agents' patterns of choice. | The same as in drama, but including agents of both human and computer origin. |
| **Thought** | Inferred internal processes leading to choice: cognition, emotion, and reason. | The same as in drama, but including processes of both human and computer origin. |
| **Language** | The selection and arrangement of words; the use of language. | The selection and arrangement of signs, including verbal, visual, auditory, and other nonverbal phenomena when used semiotically. |
| **Melody (Pattern)** | Everything that is heard, but especially the melody of speech. | The pleasurable perception of pattern in sensory phenomena. |
| **Spectacle (Enactment)** | Everything that is seen. | The sensory dimensions of the action being represented: visual, auditory, kinesthetic and tactile, and potentially all others. |

*Table 2.1* **The six qualitative elements of structure in drama and in human-computer activity.**

## Enactment

Aristotle described the fundamental material element of drama as "spectacle"—all that is seen. In the *Poetics*, he also

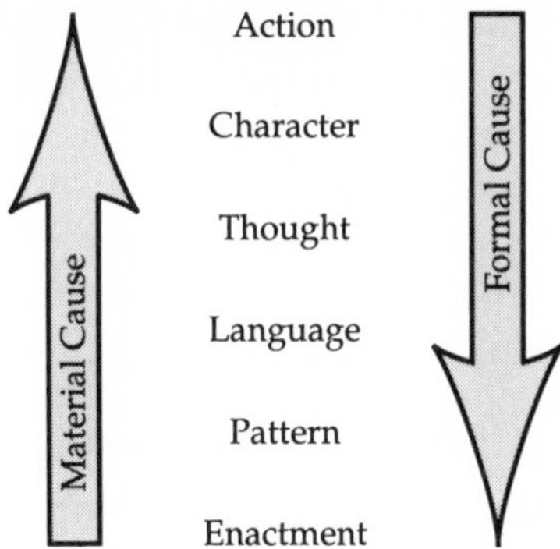


*Figure 2.2* **Causal relations among elements of quantitative structure.**

referred to this element as "performance," which provides some basis for expanding the definition to include other senses as well. Some scholars place the auditory sense in the second level because of its association with music and melody, but, as will be seen in the next section, it is more likely that the notion of melody pertains to the *patterning* of sound rather than to the auditory channel itself.

One difference, probably temporary, between drama and human-computer activity is the senses that are addressed in the enactment.[4] Traditionally, plays are available only to the eyes and ears; we cannot touch, smell, or taste them. There are interesting exceptions. In the 1920s, for instance, director David Belasco experimented with using odors as part of the performance of realistic plays; it is said that he abandoned this approach when he observed that the smell of bacon frying utterly distracted the audience from the action on stage. In the mid-1960s, Morton Heilig invented a stand-alone

[4]Aristotle defined the enactment in terms of the audience rather than the actors. Although actors employ movement (kinesthetics) in their performance of the characters, that movement is perceived visually—the audience has no direct kinesthetic experience. Likewise, although things may move about on a computer screen, a human user may or may not be having a kinesthetic experience.

arcade machine called Sensorama, which provided stereoscopic filmic images, kinesthetic feedback, and environmental smells—for example, on a motorcycle ride through New York City, the audience could smell car exhaust fumes and pizza. Sensorama's problem was not that it addressed the wrong senses; it simply happened at a time when the business community couldn't figure out what to do with it—pinball parlors were monolithic, and it would be several years before *Pong* kicked off the arcade game industry.

At the same time that Heilig was thinking about multisensory arcade games and movie theatres, the development of new genres of participatory theatre accelerated. Such artists as Judith Melina and Julian Beck of the Living Theatre, Robert Wilson, Peter Brook, Jerzy Grotowski, and John Cage experimented with performances that began to dissolve the boundaries between actors and audience by placing both in the same space. Wilson, Cage, Josef Svoboda, and others produced works that integrated filmic and photographic images, musical instruments, and machines in novel ways.

In the 1980s, these trends toward increasing the sensory dimensions of audience participation gave rise to works where the audience could touch the actors and scenery and move about freely in the performance space. For example, in *Tina and Tony's Wedding*, a contemporary "interactive" play, the audience is invited to follow the actors around from room to room (kinesthetic), to touch props and sit on the furniture (tactile and kinesthetic), and to share in a wedding banquet (taste and smell). Another notable example is Chris Hardman's Antenna Theatre, where audience members move around a set prompted by taped dialogue and narration heard through personal headphones. A spate of site-specific interactive plays and "mystery weekends" in the late 1980s enjoyed a fair amount of commercial success. Contemporary performance art shares many of the same origins.

It is interesting that the development of this theatrical genre has been concurrent with the blossoming of computer games as a popular form of entertainment, and I speculate that computer games have in some ways served as a model for it. In fact, it is in the areas that dramatic entertainment and human-computer activity are beginning to converge that pan-sensory representation is being most actively explored. When we examine that convergence, we can see ways in which human-computer activity has evolved, at least in part, as drama's attempt to increase its sensory bandwidth, creating the technological siblings of the kind of participatory theatre described above.

The notion of "interactive movies," which has gained popularity in the late 1980s, has its roots in both cinema and computer games, two forms that combine theatre and technology. Earlier works were relatively isolated. These include the productions of Lanterna Magica in Czechoslovakia and an "interactive movie" that was shown in the Czech Pavilion at the 1967 World Expo in Montreal, Canada, in which the audience was allowed to influence the course of the action by selecting from among several alternatives at a few key points in the film (however, it is rumored that all roads led to Rome—that is, all paths through the movie led to the same ending). The idea of interactive movies has been rekindled and transformed into a bona fide trend by advances in multimedia technology. Likewise, there were early experiments in interactive television in the mid-1970s (such as the failed Warner QUBE system). Interactive TV had to await similar technological advances before finally becoming a 1990s buzz-word.

In drama, the use of technology to create representations goes at least as far back as the *mechane* of the ancient Greeks. Cinema as a distinct form diverged from drama as the result of the impact of a new performance technology on form, structure, and style. In complementary fashion, computer games can be seen to have evolved from the impact of dramatic ideas on the technology of interactive computing and graphical displays. Computer games incorporate notions about character and action, suspense and empathy, and other aspects of dramatic representation.[5] Almost from the begin-

[5]Within the art of computer games, there are various forms, including action games, strategy games, adventure games, and so on.

ning, they have involved the visual, auditory, and kinesthetic senses (you need only watch a game player with a joystick to see the extent to which movement is involved, both as a cause and effect of the representation).

At the blending point of cinema and computer games are such new forms as super-arcade games like *Battle Tech* and sensory-rich amusement park installations like *Star Tours*. These types of systems involve the tactile and kinesthetic senses; some are investigating the inclusion of the other senses as well through both performance technology and direct stimulation to the nervous system [Rosen and Gosser, 1987]. "Virtual reality" systems, which are discussed in Chapter 6, increase intensity through techniques described as *sensory immersion*—instead of looking at a screen, for instance, a person is surrounded by stereoscopic sounds and visual images delivered through earphones and "eyephones." Through the use of special input devices like specially instrumented gloves and suits, people may move about and interact directly with objects in a virtual world. Interestingly, the first virtual reality systems and applications were developed for nonentertainment purposes like computer-aided design, scientific visualization, and training. Home computers and home game systems are not far behind these expensive, special-purpose systems in their ability to deliver multisensory representations.

The element of enactment is composed of all of the sensory phenomena that are part of the representation. Because of the evolutionary processes described above, it seems appropriate to say that enactment can potentially involve all of the senses. These sensory phenomena are the basic material of both drama and human-computer activity; they are the clay that is progressively shaped by the creator, whether playwright or designer.

## Pattern

The perception of patterns in sensory phenomena is a source of pleasure for humans. Aristotle described the second element of drama as "melody," a kind of pattern in the realm of sound. In the *Poetics* he says that "melody is the greatest of the pleasurable accessories of tragedy" [*Poetics*, 1450b, 15–17]. The orthodox view is that "spectacle" is the visual dimension and "melody" is the auditory one, but this view is problematic in the context of formal and material causality. If the material cause of all sounds (music) were things that could be perceived by the eye (spectacle), then things like the vibration of vocal cords and the melodies of off-stage musicians would be excluded. On the contrary, all that is seen in a play is not shaped solely by the criterion of producing sounds or music (although this may have been more strictly true in the performance style of the ancient Greeks than it is today). The formal-material relationship does not work within the context of these narrow definitions of music and spectacle.

In the previous section, we have already expanded spectacle into all sensory elements of the enactment. The notion of melody as the arrangement of sounds into a pleasing pattern can be extended analogically to the arrangement of visual images, tactile or kinesthetic sensations, and probably smells and tastes as well (as a good chef can demonstrate). In fact, the idea that a pleasurable pattern can be achieved through the arrangement of visual or other sensory materials can be derived from other aspects of the *Poetics*, so its absence here is something of a mystery. Looking "up" the hierarchy, it could be that Aristotle did not see the visual as a potentially semiotic or linguistic medium, and hence narrowed the causal channel to lead exclusively to spoken language. Whatever the explanation, the orthodox view of Aristotle's definitions of spectacle and melody leaves out too much material. As scholars are wont to do, I will blame the vagaries of translation, figurative language, and mutations introduced by centuries of interpretation for this apparent lapse and proceed to advocate my own view.

The element of pattern thus refers to patterns in the sensory phenomena of the enactment. These patterns exert a formal influence on the enactment, just as semiotic usage formally influences patterns. A key point that Aristotle made is that patterns are pleasurable to perceive in and of themselves, whether or not they are further formulated into semiotic devices or language; he spoke of them, not only as the material for language, but also as "pleasurable accessories." Hence the use of pattern as a source of pleasure is a characteristic of dramatic representations, and one which can comfortably be extended to the realm of human-computer experience.

## Language

The element of *language* (usually translated as diction) in drama is defined by Aristotle as "the expression of their [the characters'] thought in words" [*Poetics*, 1450b, 12–15]. Hence the use of spoken language as a system of signs is distinguished from other theatrical signs like the use of gesture, color, scenic elements, or paralinguistic elements (patterns of inflection and other vocal qualities). In the orthodox view, diction refers only to words—their choice and arrangement. That definition presents some interesting problems in the world of human-computer activities, many of which involve no words at all (e.g., most skill-and-action computer games, as well as graphical adventure games and graphical simulations). Are there elements in such nonverbal works that can be defined as *language*?

When a play is performed for a deaf audience and signing is used, few would argue that those visual signs function as language. The element of language in this case is expressed in a way that takes into account the sensory modalities available to the audience.[6] A designer may choose, for whatever reason, to build a human-computer system that neither senses nor responds to words, and which uses no words in the representation. Hardware configurations without keyboards, speech recognition, or text display capabilities may be unable to work with words.

[6]It is interesting to note in this context that American Sign Language (ASL) is in fact a "natural language" in its own right, and not a direct gestural map of English or any other spoken language. If a language can be constructed from gesture, then it follows that spoken words are not essential elements of language.

In human-computer activities, graphical signs and symbols, nonverbal sounds, or animation sequences may be used in the place of words as the means for explicit communication between computers and people. Such nonverbal signs may be said to function as language when they are the principal medium for the expression of thought. Accordingly, the selection and arrangement of those signs may be evaluated in terms of the same criteria as Aristotle specified for diction—for example, the effective expression of thought and appropriateness to character.

## Thought

The element of *thought* in drama may be defined as the processes leading to a character's choices and actions—for example, to emotion, cognition, reason, and intention. Understood in this way, the element of thought "resides" within characters, although it can be described and analyzed in aggregate form (the element of *thought* in a given play may be described as concerned with certain specific ethical questions, for example). Although it may be explicitly expressed in the form of dialogue, thought is *inferred*, by both the audience and the other characters (agents), from a character's choices and actions. In his application of a theatrical analogy to the domain of artificial intelligence, Julian Hilton puts it this way: "What the audience does is supply the inferencing engine which drives the plot, obeying Shakespeare's injunction to eke out the imperfections of the play (its incompleteness) with its mind." [Hilton, 1991]

If we extend this definition of thought to include human-computer activities, it leads to a familiar conundrum: Can computers think? There is an easy answer. Computer-based agents, like dramatic characters, do not have to *think* (in fact, there are many ways in which they cannot); they simply have to *provide a representation from which thought may be inferred.*

When a folder on my Macintosh desktop opens to divulge its contents in response to my double-click, the representation succeeds in getting me to infer that that's exactly what happened—that is, the "system" understood my input, inferred *my* purpose, and did what I wanted. Was the system (or the folder) "thinking" about things this way? The answer, I think, is that it doesn't matter. The real issue is that the representation succeeded in getting me to make the right inferences about its "thoughts." It also succeeded in representing to me that it made the right inferences about mine!

Thought is the formal cause of language; it shapes what an agent communicates through the selection and arrangement of signs, and thus also has a formal influence on pattern and enactment. The traditional explanation of how language serves as material for thought is based on the overly limiting assumption that agents employ language, or the language-like manipulation of symbols, in the process of thinking. This assumption leads to the idea that characters in a play use the language of the play quite literally as the material for their thoughts.

I favor a somewhat broader interpretation of material causality: *The thought of a play can appropriately deal only with what is already manifest at the levels of enactment, pattern, and language.* Most of us have seen plays in which characters get ideas "out of the blue"—suddenly remembering the location of a long-lost will, for instance, or using a fact to solve a mystery that has been withheld from the audience thus far. The above theory would suggest that the interjection of such thoughts is unsatisfying (and mars the play) because they are not drawn from the proper material. Plays, like human-computer activities, are closed universes in the sense that they delimit the set of potential actions. As we will see in the discussion of action below, it is key to the success of a dramatic representation that all of the materials that are formulated into action are drawn from the circumscribed potential of the particular dramatic world. Whenever this principle is violated, the organic unity of the work is diminished, and the scheme of probability that holds the work together is disrupted.

This principle can be demonstrated to apply to the realm of human-computer activity as well. One example is the case in which the computer (a computer-based agent) introduces new materials at the level of thought—"out of the blue." Suppose a new word processor is programmed to be constantly checking for spelling errors and to automatically correct them as soon as they are identified. If the potential for this behavior is not represented to you in some way, it will be completely disruptive when it occurs, and it will probably cause you to make seriously erroneous inferences, to perhaps think "something is wrong with my fingers, my keyboard, or my computer." The computer "knows" why it did what it did ("thought" exists) but you do not; correct inferences cannot be made.[7] A text message, for instance, or an animation of a dictionary with its pages turning (language), could represent the action as it is occurring.

Other kinds of failures in human-computer activity can also be seen as failures on the level of thought. One of my favorite examples is a parser used in several text adventure games. This particular parser did not "know" all of the words that were used in the text representation of the story. So a person might read the sentence, "Hargax slashed the dragon with his broadsword." The person might then type, "take the broadsword," and the "game" might respond, "`I DON'T KNOW THE WORD 'BROADSWORD'.`" The inference that one would make is that the game "agent" is severely brain-damaged, since the agent that produces language and the agent that comprehends it are assumed to be one in the same. This is the converse of the problem described in the last paragraph; rather than "knowing" more than it represented, the agent represented more than it "knew." Both kinds of errors are attributable to a glitch in the formal-material relationship between language and thought.

---

[7]In human factors discourse, this type of failure is attributed to a failure to establish the correct conceptual model of a given system [see Rubinstein and Hersh, 1984, Chapter 5]. The dramatic perspective differs slightly from this view by suggesting that proper treatment of the element of thought can provide a good "conceptual model" for the entire medium. It also avoids the potential misuse of conceptual models as personal constructs that "explain" what is "behind" the representation—that is, how the computer or program actually "works."

## Character and Agency

Aristotle maintained that the *object* of (i.e., what is being imitated by) a drama is action, not persons: "We maintain that Tragedy is primarily an imitation of action, and that it is mainly for the sake of the action that it imitates the personal agents" (*Poetics*, 1450b, 1–5). In drama, *character* may be defined as bundles of traits, predispositions, and choices that, when taken together, form coherent entities. Those entities are the agents of the action represented in the plot. This definition emphasizes the primacy of action.

In order to apply the same definition to human-computer activities, we must demonstrate first that agents are in fact part of such representations, and second, that there are functional and structural similarities between such agents and dramatic characters.

In a purely Aristotelian sense, an agent is one who takes action. Interestingly, Aristotle admits of the possibility of a play without characters, but a play without action cannot exist [*Poetics*, 1450a, 22–25]. This suggests that agency as part of a representation need not be strictly embodied in "characters" as we normally think of them—that is, as representations of humans. Using the broadest definition, all computer programs that perform actions that are perceived by people can be said to exhibit agency in some form. The real argument is whether that agency is a "free-floating" aspect of what is going on, or whether it is captured in "entities"—coalesced notions of the sources of agency.

The answer, I believe, is that even when representations do not explicitly include such entities, their existence is implied. At the grossest level, people simply attribute agency to the computer itself ("I did this, and then the computer did that"). They also attribute agency to application programs ("My word processor trashed my file"). They often distinguish between the agency of system software and applications ("Multifinder crashed Excel"). They attribute agency to smaller program elements and/or their representations ("The spelling checker in my word processor found an error").

In social and legal terms, an agent is one who is empowered to act on behalf of another. This definition has been used as part of the definition of agents in the mimetic world. It implies that, beyond simply performing actions, computer-based agents perform a special kind of actions—namely, actions undertaken on behalf of people. It therefore also implies that some sort of implicit or explicit communication must occur between person and system in order for the person's needs and goals to be inferred. I think that this definition is both too narrow and too altruistic. There may be contexts in which it is useful to create a computer-based agent whose "goals" are orthogonal or even inimical to those of human agents—for instance, in simulations of combat or other situations that involve conflicting forces. Agents may also work in an utterly self-directed manner, offering the results of their work up to people after the fact.

Other criteria that have been applied to interface agents (such as anthropomorphism) will be treated in the section on agents in Chapter 5. For now, we will use the broader definition of agents to apply to human-computer activity: entities that can initiate and perform actions. Like dramatic characters, they consist of bundles of traits or predispositions to act in certain ways.

Traits circumscribe the actions (or kinds of actions) that an agent has the capability to perform, thereby defining the agent's potential. There are two kinds of traits: traits that determine how an agent can act (internal traits) and traits that represent those internal predispositions (external traits). People must be given cues by the external representation of an agent that allow them to infer its internal traits. Why? Because traits function as a kind of *cognitive shorthand* that allows people to predict and comprehend agents' actions [see Laurel, 1990]. Inferred internal traits are a component of both dramatic probability (an element of plot, as described in Chapter 3) and "ease of use" (especially in terms of the minimization of human errors) in human-computer systems. Part of the art of creating both dramatic characters and computer-based agents is the art of selecting and representing external traits that accurately reflect the agent's potential for action.

Aristotle outlined four criteria for dramatic characters that can also be applied to computer-based agents [*Poetics*, 1454a, 15–40]. The first criterion is that characters be "good" (sometimes translated as "virtuous"). Using the Aristotelian definition of "virtue," good characters are those who successfully fulfill their function—that is, those who successfully formulate thought into action. Good characters *do* (action) what they *intend* to do (thought). They also do what their creator intends them to do in the context of the whole action. The second criterion is that characters be "appropriate" to the actions they perform; that is, that there is a good match between a character's traits and what they do. The third criterion is the idea that characters be "like" reality in the sense that there are causal connections between their thoughts, traits, and actions. This criterion is closely related to dramatic probability. The fourth criterion is that characters be "consistent" throughout the whole action; that is, that a character's traits should not change arbitrarily. The mapping of these criteria to computer-based agents is quite straightforward.

Finally, we need to summarize the formal and material relationships between character and the elements above and below it in the hierarchy. Formal causality suggests that it is action, and action alone, that *shapes* character; that is, a character's traits are dictated by the exigencies of the plot. To include traits in the representation that are not manifest in action violates this principle. Material causality suggests that the stuff of which a character is made must be present on the level of thought and, by implication, language and enactment as well. A good example is the interface agent, Phil, who appears in an Apple promotional video entitled "The Knowledge Navigator" (© 1988 by Apple Computer, Inc.). In the original version, Phil was portrayed by an actor in video format. He appeared to be human, alive, and responsive at all times. But because he behaved and spoke quite simply and performed relatively simple tasks, many viewers of the video complained that he was a stupid character. His physical traits (high-resolution, real-time human portrayal) did not match his language capabilities, his thoughts, or his actions (simple tasks performed in a rather unimaginative manner). In a later version, Phil's representation was changed to a simple line-drawn cartoon character with very limited animation. People seemed to find the new version of Phil much more likable. The simpler character was more consistent and more appropriate to the action.

## The Whole Action

Representations are normally thought of as having objects, even though those objects need not be things that can or do exist in the real world. Likewise, plays are often said to represent their characters; that is, *Hamlet* is a representation of the king of Denmark, and so on. In the Aristotelian view, the object of a dramatic representation is not character but action; *Hamlet* represents the action of a man attempting to discover and punish his father's murderer. The characters are there because they are required in order to represent the action, and not the other way around. An action is made up of incidents that are causally and structurally related to one another. The individual incidents that make up *Hamlet*—Hamlet fights with Laertes, for instance—are only meaningful insofar as they are woven into the action of the mimetic whole. The form of a play is manifest in the pattern created by the arrangement of incidents within the whole action.

Another definitional property of plot is that the whole action must have a beginning, a middle, and an end. The value of beginnings and endings is most clearly demonstrated by the lack of them. The feeling produced by walking into the middle of a play or movie or being forced to leave the theatre before the end is generally unpleasant. Viewers are rarely happy when, at the end of a particularly suspenseful television program, "to be continued" appears on the screen. My favorite Macintosh example is an error message that I sometimes encounter while running Multifinder: "Excel (or some other application) has unexpectedly quit." "Well," I usually reply, "the capricious little bastard!" Providing graceful beginnings and endings for human-computer activities is most often a nontrivial problem—how to "jump-start" a database engine, for example, or how to complete a network communications session. Two rules of thumb for good beginnings is that the potential for action in that particular universe is effectively laid out, and that the first incidents in the action set up promising lines of probability for future actions. A good ending provides not only completion of the action being represented but also the kind of emotional closure that is implied by the notion of catharsis, as discussed in Chapter 3.

A final criterion that Aristotle applied to plot is the notion of magnitude:

> To be beautiful, a living creature, and every whole made up of parts, but also be of a certain definite magnitude. Beauty is a matter of size and order . . . . Just in the same way, then, as a beautiful whole made up of parts, or a beautiful living creature, must be of some size, but a size to be taken in by the eye, so a story or Plot must be of some length, but of a length to be taken in by the memory [*Poetics*, 1450b, 34–40].

The action must not be so long that you forget the beginning before you get to the end, since you must be able to perceive it as a whole in order to fully enjoy it. This criterion is most immediately observable in computer games, which may require you to be hunched over a keyboard for days on end if you are to perceive the whole at one sitting, a feat of which only teenagers are capable. Similar errors in magnitude are likely to occur in other forms, such as virtual reality systems, where the raw capabilities of a system to deliver material of seemingly infinite duration is not yet tempered by a sensitivity to the limits of human memory and attention span, or to the relationship of beauty and pleasure to duration in time-based arts.

Problems in magnitude can also plague other, more "practical" applications as well. If achievable actions with distinct beginnings and ends cannot occur within the limits of memory or attention, then the activity becomes an endless chore. On the contrary, if the granularity of actions is too small and those actions cannot be grouped into more meaningful, coherent units (such as a word processor that only lets you type or a spreadsheet that only lets you add up columns of numbers), then the activity becomes an endless stream of meaningless chores. These problems are related to the *shape* of the action as well as its magnitude, the first subject to be treated in Chapter 3.

The notion of beauty that drives Aristotle's criterion of magnitude is the idea that made things, like plays, can be organic wholes—that the beauty of their form and structure can approach that of natural organisms in the way the parts fit perfectly together. In this context, he expresses the criterion for inclusion of any given incident in the plot or whole action:

> An imitation of an action must represent one action, a complete whole, with its several incidents so closely connected that the transposal or withdrawal of any one of them will disjoin and dislocate the whole. For that which makes no perceptible difference by its presence or absence is no real part of the whole [*Poetics*, 1451a, 30–35].

If we aim to design human-computer activities that are—dare we say—*beautiful*, this criterion must be used in deciding, for instance, what a person should be required to do, or what a computer-based agent should be represented as doing, in the course of the action.

In this chapter, we have described the essential causes of human-computer activity—that is, the forces that shape it—and its qualitative elements. In the next chapter, we will consider the orchestration of action more closely, both in terms of its structure and its powers to evoke emotional and intellectual response.

Chapter Three

# Dramatic Foundations, Part II: Orchestrating Action

## Dramatic Potential: The "Flying Wedge"

What is possible in a given representational "world"? In drama—on the stage, in film, or even on television—discovering what is possible is a twofold source of pleasure for audiences. First is the stimulation to imagination and emotion that is created by carefully crafted uncertainty. (My husband and I often argue that television can be quite interactive. When we watch a show together, the interaction is the banter between us as we try to predict various plot incidents. Guests tend to find this behavior annoying.) Second is the satisfaction provided by closure when the action is complete, if the plot has been successfully constructed. When representational "worlds" are interactive, whether they be avant-garde theatre productions or virtual offices, how people find the edges of the universe—discovering what is possible—is a central issue in design. This chapter deals with how plots—representational actions—are constructed so that they provide emotional and intellectual satisfaction, and how these dramatic principles can inform the design of human-computer activity.

The action of a play consists of a series of incidents that are causally related to one another. Those incidents are specified in the script and enacted by actors in performance. In the previous chapter, we likened a computer program to the script of a play, with one important difference: Whereas the action specified in a given script will not change from performance to performance,[1] a program can lead to actions (composed of incidents) that can vary widely from session to session, depending upon the choices made and actions performed by human agents. In other words, programs generally contain more *potential* for action than plays. To understand the implications of this fact, we need to explore the nature of dramatic potential and how it is formulated into action.

The dictionary defines *potential* as something that can develop or become actual. Dramatic potential refers to the set of actions that might occur in the course of a play, as seen from the perspective of any given point in time (that is, a location along the axis of time, as the action of the play unfolds). At the beginning of a play, that set is very large—in fact, virtually anything can happen. From the instant that the first ray of light falls on the set, even perhaps before an actor has entered the scene or spoken a single word, the set of potential actions begins to narrow. What could happen begins to be constrained by what actually does happen—the lights reveal a room in a Victorian house or a fantastic heath, for example, and a banker or a fairy walks onto the stage. The actions of the characters form incidents—coherent units of action—that begin to constrain further what may follow. As incident follows upon incident and patterns of cause and effect begin to be perceived, rough notions of the shape of the whole action begin to emerge; that is, people in the audience begin to have expectations about what is to come in terms of the overall plot. Where is the play going, and what is it essentially "about"?

---

[1]Again, there are exceptions, such as the interactive plays mentioned in Chapter 2. Another example is Ayn Rand's play *Night of January 16th* [1968]. The action represented is a trial and audience members perform the roles of the jurors. The jury provides the verdict, which becomes part of the plot.

In Aristotelian terms, the potential of a play, as it progresses over time, is formulated by the playwright into a set of *possibilities*. The number of new possibilities introduced falls off radically as the play progresses. Every moment of the enactment affects those possibilities, eliminating some and making some more *probable* than others. When we learn, for instance, that Hamlet's father was murdered, it becomes probable that Hamlet will try to discover the identity of the murderer. Later in the play, it becomes probable that, once he has found the villain out, Hamlet will seek revenge. But will he succeed? At each stage of the plot, the audience can perceive more than one line of probability (that is, more than one probable course of events), creating engagement and varying degrees of suspense in the audience. At the final moment of a play (or at the peak of its "climax," as described later in this chapter), all of the competing lines of probability are eliminated except one, and that one is the final outcome. At the climactic moment of *Hamlet*, the only remaining probability is that he will die and Fortinbras will restore order to the kingdom. In this moment—the moment when probability becomes necessity—the whole action of the play is complete. Thus, over time, dramatic potential is formulated into possibility, probability, and necessity.[2]

This process can be visualized (highly schematically) as the "flying wedge" in Figure 3.1. How this pattern is accomplished in a play depends, in the main, upon the playwright's selection and arrangement of incidents and how they are causally linked. Reading the diagram from left to right shows the progression of material causality, by the way, and reading it from right to left shows formal causality at work, where the necessary end of a whole action functions as a kind of magnet, drawing the structure of the action toward itself.

The shape of potential over time in human-computer activities is similar to the flying wedge. In a play, the result of this successive formulation is a completed plot—a *whole*

[2]In the context of drama and as used in this book, the terms *possibility*, *probability*, and *necessity* have specific meanings that differ substantially from mathematical or scientific usage. Readers who wish to investigate the dramatic connotations further should review the *Poetics*, 1451a-b.

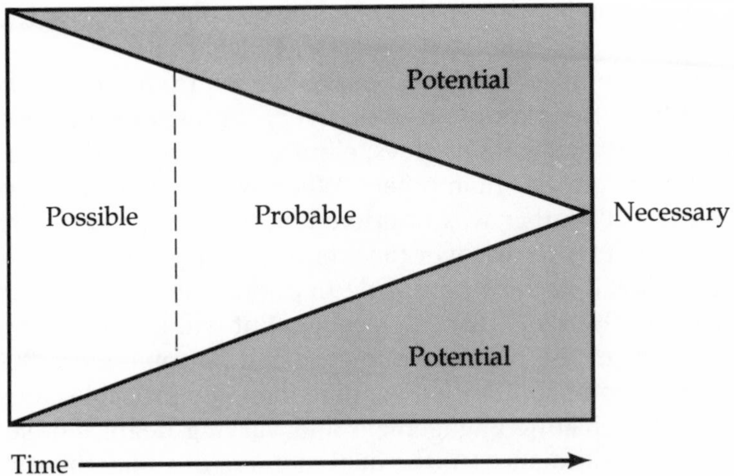


*Figure 3.1* **The "flying wedge."** A plot is a progression from the possible to the probable to the necessary.

*action*. What is the human-computer equivalent? A "whole" human-computer activity can be described, using the broad definition of a whole action, as having a beginning, middle, and end, and being composed of incidents (one or more) that are parts of that whole. Thus playing a computer game until it ends (or I end it) is a whole action, and a "session" with my word processor is a whole action (even if I don't finish the chapter I'm writing).

The notion of beginning, middle, and end presents an interesting riddle when using a computer with a multitasking operating system, or even launching and relaunching various applications in a sequential fashion. I may have several "activities" going on at once, leaping from one to another in midstream. I am using my word processor to work on an article, to send and receive electronic mail, to draw pictures, and to play a game. Where is the whole?

One answer is, to quote the famous turtle, "it's actions all the way up"—that is, several whole actions are being braided into an even larger one, which is itself a whole, with all the associated formal and structural characteristics. The upper limit of this recursion is supplied, in part, by the notion of magnitude (something of a size that can be perceived as a whole) and in part by the context(s) of activity. While working on this book, for instance, all of the actions I undertake (and all of the applications I launch) during a session with the computer are typically related to the activity of authoring the book. To the extent that the Macintosh environment supplies a consistent operational context (the "Mac interface"), consistent "tools" (such as cut and paste), and some transportability (such as the ability to bring a MacPaint image into a Microsoft Word file), the system reinforces this sense of wholeness. This idea will be expanded upon in Chapter 6.

On the other hand, I may simply boot up the computer and diddle around with various tasks—e-mail correspondence, journal entries, designing party invitations, or what-have-you. The artificial bracketing events of turning the computer on and off are not equivalent to the beginning and end of a whole action; rather, there are several "whole actions" being pursued concurrently. The possibility of multiple whole actions being undertaken in a multitasking fashion is not unique to computing; the same phenomenon occurs in the typical day of any office worker or homemaker, and it is quite familiar to the sort of reader who has several books going at once, reading science fiction in bed and journal articles in the bathroom. The point here is not to assert that there is necessarily a single whole action being constructed every time that a person uses a computer, but rather to suggest that the quality of wholeness has contextual, structural, and formal characteristics.

Whatever the duration or scale, human-computer activities can be seen to formulate potential in the same way that drama does—as a progression from possibility to probability to necessity. The opening display (which may or may not be multisensory) begins the process of delimiting potential. Every action taken by an agent, including the human agent(s), creates further possibilities and constraints as the activity takes shape. Thinking about things this way helps us to focus on how incidents can be arranged and causally linked. A human-computer activity, unlike a play, may be formulated uniquely every time it is performed. The source of variability is people, through their choices and actions, which in turn reflect different goals, styles, and capabilities (Figure 3.2).

Many of the aspects of a play's *enactment* are the result of the rehearsal process, where the director and/or actors determine where and when to move and what sorts of lighting and other technical effects should be produced. If these inventions were happening in real time rather than in the rehearsal process, plays could be seen as being far more "dynamic" in terms of the enactors' relationship to the script. The displacement is temporal, but so are the constraints. The thing that actors and directors typically cannot do is to change the order of events or the words spoken by the characters, either in rehearsal or performance, nor can they invent new ones. A program that reformulates the potential for action, creating new possibilities and probabilities "on the fly" as a response to what has gone before, is equivalent to a playwright chang-

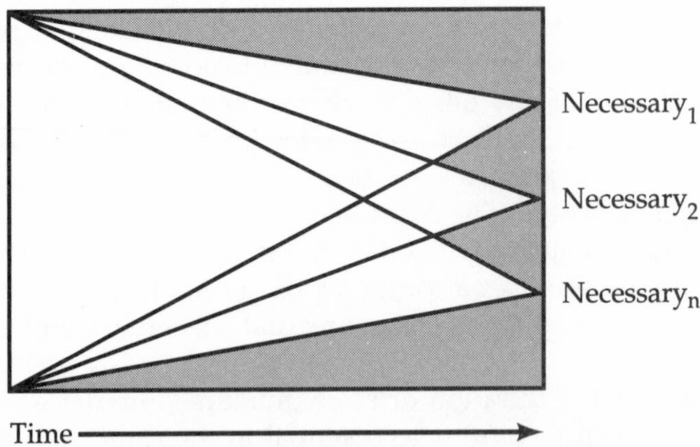


*Figure 3.2* **The "flying wedge" in interactive forms.** In human-computer activity, the shaping of potential is influenced by people's real-time choices and actions, pruning possibilities and creating lines of probability that differ from session to session and person to person. The "flying wedge" can be pointed off in different directions, thus increasing the program's potential for many whole actions.

ing a plot in real time as a collaboration with the actors and director, and communicating new portions of script to them in real time through some automagical means. In other words, the way in which human-computer activity is more dynamic than drama is in the aspect of formulating the action (playwriting) rather than in its enactment (performance).

But humans can theoretically introduce anything they like into the potential of a given human-computer activity! Introducing new potential, especially "late in the game," has the capacity to explode the structure of the action. How can people be constrained to work only with potential that is inherent in (or amenable to) that which is already in the representational world? The problem of *constraints* is treated later in this chapter, but a key element in its solution is the deployment of dramatic probability and causality to indirectly guide what people think of doing.

## Probability and Causality

Causality is the connective tissue of plot.[3] In this context, causality refers to the cause-and-effect relationships within the action that is being represented. The causal relationship of an incident to the whole action is a requirement for inclusion. Causality also determines, in part, where an incident will be placed in the plot—causes are sometimes represented after effects, for instance, for the purpose of orchestrating audience response through such means as suspense and surprise. Incidents are said to be "gratuitous" if they have no causal relationship to the whole action; gratuitous incidents shed no light on why things have happened or why they happened as

---

[3]The notion of causality contains some cultural bias; that is, the notion of cause and effect is not as universal as Aristotle believed. Some cultures substitute temporal relations for causal ones, for instance. Likewise, many avant-garde playwrights of the twentieth century, especially the absurdists and surrealists, attempted to eliminate linear causality from dramatic structure. In the main, however, the notion of causality is pervasive and robust enough to justify our use of it as the basis of our theory. Of course, other theories might (and probably should) be formulated from the alternative views of other cultures and philosophies.

they did; they may also be the effects of causes that are not represented.

Gratuitous incidents have no direct bearing on the plot; for example, there is no reason to include a scene where Hamlet brushes his teeth. Most of us have been annoyed by gratuitous incidents in films and TV shows, and many of us have been annoyed by the same kinds of incidents in human-computer activities. A convention in the world of computer-aided instruction (CAI), for instance, is to ask the student to enter his or her name at the beginning of an interactive session. Typically, the computer "responds" with a text-based reply, "Hello there, Jimmy," and then abruptly terminates this seemingly friendly greeting ritual as the program lurches into the "meat" of the lesson. The name-entering incident (Jimmy and the computer say "hi") has nothing to do with the plot (Jimmy learns his multiplication tables).

Gratuitous incidents in human-computer activities most often occur in the presentation of extraneous information. The appearance of menus, prompts, or "helps"—presented whether you want them or not—is one common annoyance; the appearance of "garbage text" is another. The mail facility on most large systems appends a header to displayed messages that contains a cacophony of information that people need not clutter their brains (or screens) with. Information about the path that a message took between nodes in a network may be of functional use in delivering a response automatically, but its visual representation (as text headers) is usually gratuitous in terms of the *action* of using electronic mail (Figure 3.3).

Another example of gratuitous incidents are bungled efforts to provide "intrinsic motivation" in educational programs (often based upon gross misinterpretations of Malone [1980]) by interspersing problem-solving or tutorial segments with pieces of games, as illustrated by this example:

> Typing Tutor, designed to teach the use of the typewriter keyboard. This program combines practice lessons with an arcade-style game in which the student must type a displayed letter in time to "shoot down" incoming "missiles." [Horowitz, 1988]

```
From: well!hlr@apple.com (Howard Rheingold)
To: LAUREL.B@AppleLink.Apple.COM
From apple!@RELAY.CS.NET:ishii@ntthif.ntt.jp Thu
Jun 7 23:45:39 1990
Received: by well.sf.ca.us (4.12/4.7)
 id AA11768; Thu, 7 Jun 90 23:45:32 pdt
Received: from relay.cs.net by apple.com with SMTP
(5.61/25-eef)
 id AA01351; Thu, 7 Jun 90 20:56:13 -0700
 for hlr
Received: from relay2.cs.net by RELAY.CS.NET id
aa03096; 7 Jun 90 23:47 EDT
Received: from ntt.jp by RELAY.CS.NET id ab11409;
7 Jun 90 23:37 EDT
Received: by ntt-sh.ntt.jp (3.2/ntt-sh-03i) with
TCP; Fri, 8 Jun 90 12:32:20
JST
Received: by YECL.ntt.jp (1.2/NTTcs02b) with TCP;
Fri, 8 Jun 90 12:28:43+0900
Received: by nttcvg.ntt.jp (1.2/NTTcs01b) with
TCP; Fri, 8 Jun 90 12:35:24 jst
Received: by ntthif.ntt.jp (3.2/NTTcs01) with TCP;
Fri, 8 Jun 90 12:26:13 JST
Date: Fri, 8 Jun 90 12:26:13 JST
From: Hiroshi Ishii <apple!ntthif.ntt.jp!ishii>
Message-Id: <9006080326.AA03491@ntthif.ntt.jp>
```

*Figure 3.3* A particularly heinous example of an e-mail header.

This design strategy is often seen in mathematics drill-and-practice programs. If Jimmy solves three arithmetic problems successfully, he gets to spend twenty seconds playing a low-res starship-blaster-action game. Either the math or the game segments are gratuitous, depending upon Jimmy's understanding of the central action. The solution is either to eliminate one of the activities, or to reshape the action so that it includes both in a causally related way—for example, a starfighter simulation in which Jimmy solves math problems in order to operate the ship.[4]

Besides its function as a criterion for inclusion, causality is employed by playwrights in the shaping of dramatic probability. The representation of certain causes makes certain effects probable. The possibility of conflict in the Neutral Zone (part of the dramatic potential of *Star Trek*) becomes a probability if a cause is represented—for example, a Romulan incursion. In a complementary fashion, the representation of effects leads people to expect that causes will be revealed—another way of constraining what is probable.

A primary source of causality in dramatic incidents is the goals of the characters—that is, what the characters want and are trying to do. The central action of a play is often best described in terms of the goal of its central character. Characters try various courses of action for achieving their goals. The obstacles and conflicts they encounter force changes in their behaviors and plans, and sometimes in the goals themselves. A detective in a movie may start out trying to solve a murder and end up embroiled in an international espionage operation. Of course, by the end of the film, the audience can see that the action was "about" the spy ring all along, because knowing about it makes all the details fall into place. The central character's goal has carried them along, and the revelation of the other characters' goals unifies seemingly unrelated incidents into a whole action through the interweaving of causality.

Likewise, the agents' goals are most often the strongest source of causality in human-computer activity. What is each agent (human and computer-based) trying to do, get, or become? What obstacles and conflicts arise, and how do they constrain what the agents do? In human-computer activity, as in drama, goals usually lead to the formulation of plans for achieving them. These plans are either stated or inferred, and

[4]The preceding three paragraphs are modified from "Interface as Mimesis," in D. A. Norman and S. Draper, eds., *User Centered System Design: New Perspectives on Human-Computer Interaction*. Hillsdale, N.J.: Lawrence Erlbaum Associates, 1986. Reprinted with permission.

they provide a basis whereby to understand the action. The implementation, failure, revision, and formulation of plans are the "meat" of the action. To be probable, goals and plans must be plausible in terms of the characters that generate them (the "appropriateness" criterion for character, as discussed in Chapter 2).

In his dissertation, "The Dynamic Structure of Everyday Life," AI researcher Philip Agre argues that real people do not live their lives this way—that is, that goals and plans do not explain most of human behavior. His observations have led him to posit that people are primarily involved in improvising what to do next, in a moment-by-moment way, and that everyday life is "always almost wholly routine" [Agre, 1988]. But everyday life is different from drama. And highly goal-oriented "real" behavior, as in the case of constructing a building or some other specific task (the kind of thing we often do with computers), can be seen to involve a greater proportion of planning activity than "everyday life" as well. Agre's understanding of everyday activity has enabled him to arrive at AI architectures that may do a remarkable job of emulating real life, and his ideas may lead to an entirely new paradigm for representing and orchestrating human-computer activity.

Nevertheless, I employ the notions of goals and plans in this book for several reasons. One is the desire to see human-computer activities as "wholes" with coherent structures. Constructing them as *dramatic* wholes allows us to take advantage of deeply ingrained conventions about understanding representations of action. These conventions—elimination of the extraneous and gratuitous, clear causal relations among things that happen, and the notions of beginnings, middles, and ends—are in fact the ways in which drama is *not* like life. Agre wants artificial reality to be lifelike, but there are good reasons why, at least in some situations and for some purposes, artificial reality should be, well, *artificial*.

Related to Agre's thesis is the work of Lucy Suchman. In her excellent book, *Plans and Situated Actions: The Problem of Human-Machine Communication* [1987], Suchman contends that "purposeful" (or goal-directed) behavior is best understood, not as the execution of plans, but rather as *situated actions* —"actions taken in the context of particular, concrete circumstances." Plans are fundamentally ineffective because "the circumstances of our actions are never fully anticipated and are continuously changing around us." Suchman's observations have led her to conclude that plans are best viewed as "a weak resource for what is primarily *ad hoc* activity." Suchman does not deny the existence or use of plans but implies that deciding what to do next in the pursuit of some goal is a far more dynamic and context-dependent activity than the traditional notion of planning might suggest.

A dramatic view of human-computer interaction is amenable to the notion of situated actions in that it attempts to dynamically represent changing situational elements and to incorporate knowledge of them into both the decision-making processes of computer-based agents and the understanding of the actions of human agents in representational contexts. An in-depth integration of Suchman's work into a dramatic model of human-computer interaction is beyond the scope of this book, but it will be a necessary element of both the elaboration of the model and the development of future systems that attempt to instantiate it.

In keeping with Suchman's analysis is the fact that many factors dynamically influence agents' choices and actions and thereby contribute to dramatic causality—among them, natural forces, coincidences, situations, and conditions. Of course, "natural" forces represented in plays and imaginary worlds may be very different from those at work in the real world. Computer games select and modify the laws of physics, for instance. In computer-based simulations, new scientific developments such as fractal geometry and other mathematical representations of chaos theory make it possible to emulate the natural world with much greater detail and accuracy than formerly possible. However, even these techniques must be deployed selectively in the process of representation-building; attempting to render the physical world (or a comparably robust alternative) *completely* would quickly bring the world's most powerful computers (and programmers) to their (virtual) knees. Even when selectivity is not an artistic choice, it is nevertheless a necessity in computer-based modeling of physical worlds. The important thing is to know that one is in fact exercising selectivity—to be explicit about it, and to employ a notion of the *potential for action* in the world one is creating as the primary selection criteria. Representing a natural force makes certain kinds of actions more probable; for instance, simulating air flow around an aircraft wing in a CAD program suggests that changes in the wing will create changes in the air flow, implying both causality and potential action. If the potential for adjusting the wing in some way is successfully represented, then the possibility of adjustment becomes more probable.

Representations of functionality that do not model the physical world still employ equivalents of natural laws in the ways that things behave. Zoom-boxes and windows open and close with animated embellishments that suggest real-world physical actions; folders appear to exert a gravitational force within a limited area that sucks documents into them. (When the representation of such a force is flawed, the comparison with black holes in space may be unintentionally evoked.) Whether in plays, computer games, simulations, or virtual desktops, the representation of "natural" forces must be consistent and explicit enough to allow people to incorporate them into their understanding of the particular world's potential.

The construction of situations that possess strong dramatic potential is a central element in the playwright's art. Situations may have both physical and character-related components (a gun on a desk; a desire for revenge). An obvious but easily overlooked element of situation-building is the fact that all of the relevant aspects of the situation must be successfully *represented*. Watching a small child struggle with a "drawing" program on the computer is a case in point; her actions are limited by her ability to recognize the tools and the context. She is simply not able to do the kind of investigation of the environment and situation that a computer-savvy adult would be willing to undertake; she doesn't know what rocks to look under (or menus to pull down). For her, the representation is all there is.

Coincidences can also help to establish probability, but they are ineffective when they appear to be arbitrary. Outrageously arbitrary coincidences are the stuff of comedy and farce, in which the requirements for plausibility are significantly relaxed. People commonly assume that coincidences in noncomic representations *have causes that will be revealed*; that is, they are more than "random" accidents. In fact, seeming coincidences stimulate people to look for causal connections. If a sword shows up at just at the moment when I need it in the enchanted castle, is the wizard protecting me? Fortuitous events imply agency, and that is essentially what they are good for—implying the involvement of characters or forces in the action.

The fact that people seek to understand causality in representational worlds provides the basis for Aristotle's definition of *universality*. In the colloquial view, an action is universal if everybody can understand it, regardless of cultural and other differences among individuals. This would seem to limit the set of universal actions to things that everyone on the planet does—eat, sleep, love, etc. Aristotle posits that *any* action can be "universalized" simply by revealing its cause; that is, understanding the cause is sufficient for understanding the action, even if it is something alien to a person's culture, background, or personal "reality."

Works of fantasy provide an obvious example of how universalization via causality works. Actions that are patently impossible in the real world (such as a person flying) can be made believable and understandable in their dramatic context if probability is established. This fact led Aristotle to observe that in dramatic action, *an impossible probability is preferable to an improbable possibility*. We can believe that Peter Pan flies because of the way the potential of his world is revealed, through the way his character is established in the action, and through dramatic situations that provide him with causes to use his ability to fly. Conversely, it is *possible* that Peter Pan would try to have a conversation with Captain Hook instead of fighting with him (a Monty-Pythonesque treatment), but the *improbability* of that course of action robs it of credibility. This is another reason why coincidences don't work: it's improbable, in all noncomic dramatic forms, for just the right thing to happen at just the right time without some source of agency.

To summarize, probability is the key quality of dramatic action. The orchestration of probability and causality is the stuff that dramaturgy is made of. By manipulating probability, the playwright shapes the dramatic world, the plot, and the shape of the audience's involvement with it. Similarly, it can be deployed by designers of human-computer experience to shape what people do and feel in the context of a particular virtual world. To understand more about how dramatic probability can be shaped, we can look to the structural patterns that make probability manifest.

# Dramatic Anatomy

How does one describe the shape of a particular play? What are its "anatomical" parts? The previous sections dealt with qualitative elements—that is, qualities that exist throughout the fabric of a play. This section deals with the identifiable patterns through which qualitative elements are expressed.

## Complication and Resolution

The *shape* of a play can be visualized in terms of the pattern of emotional tension created in its audience. Typically, tension rises during the course of a play until the climax of the action and falls thereafter. As we observed in the previous section, the climax of a play is the moment at which one line of probability becomes necessity, and all competing lines of probability are eliminated. Hence the climax is not only an emotional peak but an informational one as well. In fact, the implicit assumption in this analysis is that there is a direct relationship between what we *know* about the action and how we *feel* about it. The manipulation of information establishes causality and probability, and it is the basis of such audience responses as suspense, surprise, and catharsis.

Gustav Freytag, a German critic and playwright, suggested in 1863 that the action of a play could be represented graphically, yielding a visualization of dramatic anatomy that is referred to as "Freytag's triangle" (Figure 3.4). The notion that the action of a play could be quantified was not unfamiliar to Freytag's contemporaries in Europe and America, whose "well-made plays" were often formulaic in the extreme (and which did not survive as examples of great drama). It is the underlying logic of Freytag's analysis, however, and not the recipe-book flavor of his techniques, that is useful in understanding the anatomy of dramatic action.

Freytag's visualization was based on the notions of rising and falling action. (Freytag's actual terms were "play" and "counter-play," and they were based on Aristotle's "complication" and "dénouement.") The *rising action* is all that leads up to a climax or turning point; the *falling action* is all that happens from the climax to the conclusion. The rising and falling action form the sides of the triangle, of which the dramatic climax is the apex. The horizontal axis of the graph is time; the

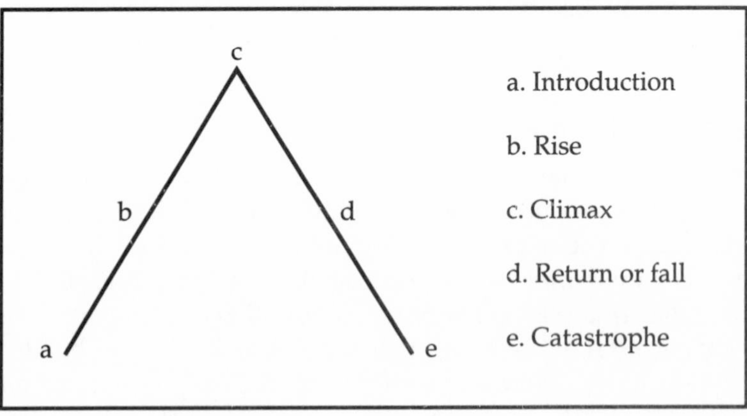


*Figure 3.4* **Freytag's triangle.**

vertical axis is complication. Various structural elements occupy different locations on the triangle. Contemporary versions of Freytag's triangle are more irregular and jagged, reflecting the differing patterns of complication and resolution within structural elements.

The "complication axis" of a Freytag triangle represents the *informational attributes* of each dramatic incident. An incident that raises questions (e.g., the kidnapping of the heroine) is part of the rising action; one that answers questions (e.g., the confession of the villain) is part of falling action. However, Freytag's analysis is overly simplistic; each dramatic incident may raise some questions and answer others, and the questions themselves may vary in importance to the plot. Freytag's primary contribution was to provide the beginnings of a visual representation of the shape of dramatic action.

More sophisticated Freytag-style graphs have been developed as tools for dramatic analysis. Each incident is represented as a line segment, the *slope* of which is derived from the relationship of the informational attributes of the incident (i.e., questions asked and answered) to its duration; for instance, a steep upward slope represents a good deal of complication in a short amount of time. We will use the following dramatic incident as an example.

A group of strangers have been invited by an anonymous person to spend the weekend in a remote mansion. During the night, one member of the group (Brown) has disappeared. Some of the remaining characters are gathered in the drawing room expressing concern and alarm. The butler (James) enters and announces that Brown has been found:

**James**: I'm afraid I have some rather shocking news.

**Smith:** Spit it out, man.

**Nancy:** Yes, can't you see my nerves are absolutely shot? If you have any information at all, you must give it to us at once.

**James:** It's about Mr. Brown.

**Smith:** Well?

**James:** We've just found him on the beach.
**Smith:** Thank heavens. Then he's all right.
**James:** I'm afraid not, sir.
**Smith:** What's that?
**James:** Actually, he's quite dead, sir.
**Nancy:** Good God! What happened?
**James:** He appears to have drowned.
**Smith:** That's absurd, man. Brown was a first-class swimmer.

Each informational component of the incident can be characterized in two ways. In terms of complication, the information is either positive (it asks a question) or negative (it answers a question). The importance of the information at the point at which it appears in the plot is rated on a numeric scale from 0 (completely unimportant) to 1 (extremely important). Thus an extremely significant piece of information that answers a question has a rating of -1, while a fairly insignificant piece of information that raises a question might have a rating of +.3. Figure 3.5 shows such an evaluation of the informational components of the incident.

| Information | Complication | Significance |
|---|---|---|
| a. James has shocking news. | + | .4 |
| b. The news concerns Brown. | + | .5 |
| c. Brown has been found. | – | .7 |
| d. Brown is dead. | + | .9 |
| e. Brown has drowned. | – | .4 |
| f. Brown was a good swimmer. | + | .8 |
| TOTAL = | + | 1.5 |

*Figure 3.5* **Informational analysis of a sample incident.**

To represent the incident on a Freytag graph, the sum of the numeric ratings shown in Figure 3.5 can be used as the value for the variable c, representing complication. The duration of the incident in minutes (or pages of script) is used as the value of the variable T, representing time. The formula for computing the slope of the line segment that will represent the incident on the graph can be expressed as: slope = c/t. In this case, c = 1.5 and t = 1. The sample incident is graphed in Figure 3.6.

This analytic technique can yield a detailed profile, represented numerically or graphically, of the *shape* of the dramatic action of a given play. The fact that this aspect of structure can be expressed quantitatively makes it potentially more amenable to computational representation. Given an informational analysis of the potential actions involved in a human-computer activity, quantitative structural criteria could be used for orchestrating those incidents into the desired overall

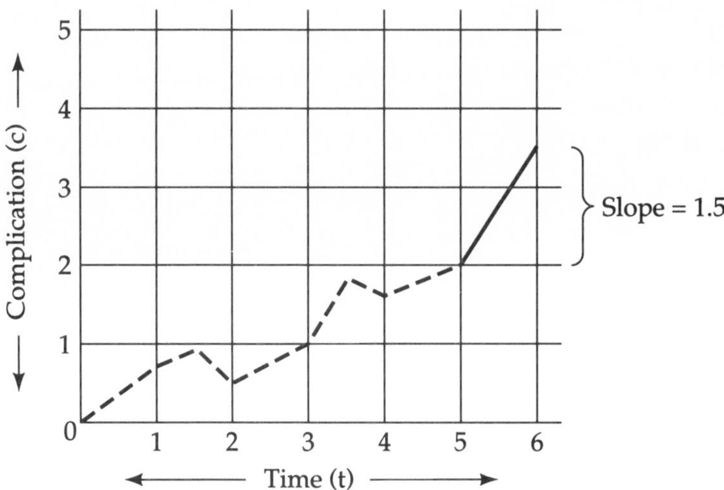


*Figure 3.6* **A "modern" Freytag-style graph.** The dashed line represents previous incidents; the solid line represents the sample incident analyzed in Figure 3.5.

*shape*. This is possible because specific kinds of actions can be seen to have characteristic slopes or curves.

## Conventional Kinds of Action

Figure 3.6 indicates five types of action, using Freytag's terms for them. These "anatomical parts" of a play have been redefined and renamed by nearly every critic since Aristotle. Today, most drama students learn a set of conventional categories and a less symmetrical (but still schematic) characteristic curve for dramatic action, shown in Figure 3.7.

The *exposition* (segment a) is the part of a play that functions to reveal the context for the unfolding action. It formulates potential into possibilities, introducing characters, environments, and situations. Exposition as the revelation of information continues throughout the play, but it diminishes as the action progresses; it becomes less and less necessary or appropriate to introduce new potential. The *inciting incident* (point b) is actually a small segment rather than a point (since it has some duration); it is the action or event that begins what will become the central action of the play. On the graph, it is the point at which the curve takes its first significant upward turn. In terms of the "flying wedge," the inciting incident initiates the first lines (vectors) of probability. The *rising action*

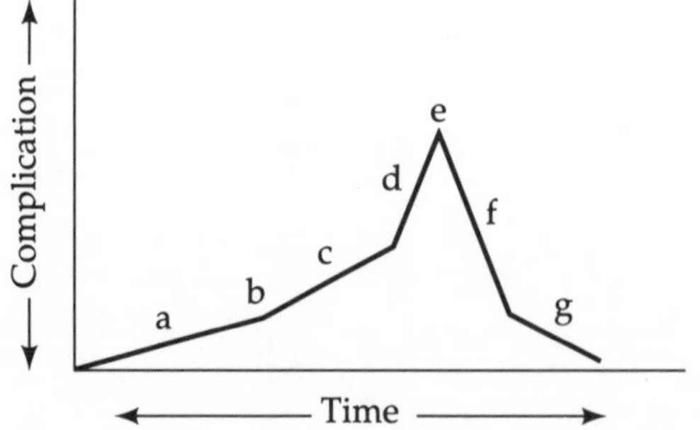


*Figure 3.7* **A more contemporary version of the shape of dramatic action and its conventionally recognized parts.**

(segment c) follows the inciting incident. In this portion of the play, the characters pursue their central goals, formulating, implementing, and revising plans, and meeting resistances and obstacles along the way. At some point, the action "goes critical"—that is, characters must make major decisions and take conclusive actions in pursuit of their goals. The *crisis* (segment d) is a period of heightened activity and commitment, and it usually proceeds at a faster pace than the preceding action. During this segment, many lines of probability are pruned away. The *climax* (point e) is the moment at which one of the lines of probability becomes necessity and all others are eliminated. Characters either succeed or fail to achieve their goals. This key incident is the turning point of the action. The *falling action* (segment f) represents the consequences of the climax, as they reverberate through character and situation. The slope of the falling action is characteristically rather steep; that is, things tend to fall into place quickly once the climax has been reached. The *dénouement* (segment g) can be described as the return to "normalcy" (the *status quo* of the dramatic world). In French, the word means "untying" or "unraveling." The dramatic potential is exhausted; its intrinsic energy has been used up by the action.

If we were to enlarge any segment of the graph for a real play, we would see (depending upon the resolution of the underlying analysis) still more bumps and curves, representing the structure of the smaller component incidents that make up the larger anatomical parts. The exposition of a play, for instance, is made up of a number of incidents that reveal information with varying c/t values. The rising action is composed of smaller incidents that tend to have a higher average slope than incidents of the exposition. Here, a fractal metaphor is apt (and perhaps it is more than a metaphor): The smaller components of a given type of action tend to reflect its structure in miniature. The overall graph of any given play is like its fingerprint; it is unique. An intriguing pastime for the quantitatively inclined is to observe how these fingerprint curves are reflected in the smaller incidents that make up larger anatomical parts. Plays can be seen to employ structural patterns in the same way that music employs themes and motifs.

An important thing to note about this analytical technique is that it reveals a major source of a play's aesthetic appeal; that is, it provides some explanation of why a play *feels good*.[5] As Aristotle's analysis of the qualitative elements of structure (discussed in Chapter 2) suggested, *pattern* is a powerful source of pleasure. Designers of human-computer activities can borrow concepts and techniques from drama in order to visualize and orchestrate the structural patterns of experience.

It is relatively easy to see the relevance of orchestrating the shape of action in story-based human-computer activities like computer games or interactive simulations. But what about more pragmatic, "computer-like" activities—say, spreadsheets? Both Heckel [1982] and Nelson [1990] have extolled the virtues of VisiCalc and its descendants. Heckel identifies one source of the product's appeal as the immediate representation of the effects of users' actions: "While entering formulas, the user is continuously stimulated. Similarly, when changing a number, the user is stimulated by the effect of the changes as they ripple through the spreadsheet" [Heckel, 1982]. This source of a good spreadsheet's appeal can be visualized as a Freytag-style curve. Let's say I'm using a spreadsheet to decide whether I can afford to buy a new house. Referring again to Figure 3.7, the various segments of the graph might correspond to the following actions:

**a.** *Getting started.* I enter the price of the desired house, the price that my current home is likely to fetch on the market, and any additional numerical data that I might have, such as interest rates, property taxes, and the costs of utilities.

---

[5]An interesting exercise in scientific (or artistic) visualization would be to create first-person versions of such graphs, so that one could experience them kinesthetically by "riding the curves." Would such abstractions *feel good* in and of themselves? If we represented them audibly, would they sound like music?

b. *Preliminary evaluation.* I discover that the new house, in terms of the data already entered, will cost me $1,000 more per month. Things are looking bad, but I really want to be able to afford the house, so now I am going to start trying to think of things that will turn the picture around. Thus the "inciting incident" is the initial set of calculations, which leads to my decision to pursue a new goal: to make the numbers support the desired outcome.
c. *Entering new data and formulas.* Are there tax benefits that derive from the interest rates and increased debt? How will my utility bills change if I replace the new house's electric heating system with a gas furnace? I try different strategies with positive and negative effects.
d. *Making major trade-offs.* Things are still looking bad to iffy; now it's time to decide what sacrifices I am willing to make. Finally I decide that I can live without a new car, that I can forgo furniture in the living room, and that I can borrow an additional chunk of down payment from my mother. Will any or all of these sacrifices be sufficient?
e. *Making the decision.* I "turn the crank" by implementing each of these sacrifice scenarios in turn and then in combination until I arrive at one I can live with. Yes, there is a way to afford the new house.
f. *Creating an artifact.* I clean up the spreadsheet, do a little formatting, and print the whole thing out to show my husband so that he, too, will be convinced.
g. *Finishing up.* I save the document and exit the application.

The spreadsheet illustrates how the conception of the application and its functionality shapes the action by providing elements of form. It also shows the way in which the application and the person collaborate to create a whole action with an interesting shape. It illustrates the fact that an application, in both its conception and its execution, defines the magnitude and texture of the whole action. Spreadsheets such as VisiCalc and Excel are successful largely because they do an extremely good job of supporting whole actions with a satisfying degree of complexity, magnitude, and completeness. You could perform the same whole action as that in the example above with a calculator, an abacus, or even a pencil and paper, but its magnitude (in the sense of duration) would be excruciatingly excessive. The action would lack organic wholeness: Rather than the elegant Freytag-like curve, the action would more likely consist of long, flat-line segments of calculation punctuated by periods of analysis and planning with a completely different representational context and "feel." In contrast, word processors, especially those that admit only of text manipulations, do a comparatively poorer job of supporting actions with interesting shapes in that they focus on only part of a larger task. In Chapter 6, we will explore the task of document creation to illustrate the application of our dramatic model.

## Discovery, Surprise, and Reversal

The previous section illustrates how information is a key component of dramatic structure. The impact that new information has on people is determined not only by the information itself but also by how it is revealed and how it interacts with existing knowledge and expectations. Plays are full of discoveries of different types. The expository action at the beginning of a play provides the greatest number of discoveries for the audience, but the climax probably provides discoveries of the greatest significance. When we have no particular expectations, discovering new information is a simple and relatively unremarkable experience (oh, I see, the door is over there; this character is a doctor; the husband and wife are having trouble getting along).

Discovery becomes more interesting when the new information is not what we might have expected—in other words, it is a surprise (What's that scruffy bum doing at this fancy party? Why is the house suddenly shaking? Will a higher interest rate give me a tax break?). Surprises have a higher potential for complication than do run-of-the-mill discoveries; that is, they often raise more questions than they answer. Although in "real" life surprises are as often nasty as they are pleasant (why is the house suddenly shaking?), in the context of *drama*, they are almost always pleasurable, in that they lead to excitement, vicarious feeling, engagement, and speculation. We are "safe" from real-world consequences. (Don't worry, honey, it's only a movie. There's no earthquake going on.) *Surprise* is that subspecies of discovery that is different from what we expected (or might logically have expected) to be true. Surprise is deployed by playwrights to turn up the gain on emotional and intellectual involvement, and to quite literally give the audience a thrill.

A rarer and more potent flavor of surprise is what Aristotle referred to as *reversal*: a surprise that reveals that the *opposite* of what we expected is true. (That's not a man, that's a *woman*! The detective is actually the murderer! I thought that "formatting" would *tidy up* my disk, not *erase* it!). Reversals can cause major changes in our understanding of what is going on and our expectations about what will happen next; in other words, they can radically alter *probability*. In a play, an early reversal might serve as an inciting incident, causing a sharp upturn in the c/t slope (by raising a whole set of questions all at once). The climax of a play may be a reversal that causes a sharp downward turn in the slope (by answering a host of questions all at once).

In human-computer activity, like drama, surprise and reversal are efficient and economical means for achieving radical shifts in probability. The reasons for wanting to create such a shift may be pragmatic or aesthetic. A reversal may be needed to turn a person away from an unproductive or potentially dangerous path of action. Surprise and reversal can also be deployed to create changes in the slope of the action in order to achieve a pleasing whole. Of course, it must be remembered that dramatic reversals have no serious real-world consequences. Obviously, one should avoid any incidents that cause actual pain or harm (such as erasing a file or destroying a document). In summary, surprises and reversals are tools for changing what people understand and expect, for stimulating interest and involvement, and for orchestrating the shape of the action.

In this chapter, we have attempted to define elements of form and structure that are characteristic of dramatic action and to relate them to human-computer activity. In the next chapter, we will consider how the dramatic theory presented in Chapters 2 and 3 can be employed to understand and orchestrate human action in representational worlds.

Chapter Four

# Dramatic Techniques for Orchestrating Human Response

## Form and Experience

The goal of the previous two chapters was to establish a groundwork in dramatic theory that involves principles of dramatic form and structure. This chapter will explore techniques for applying that theoretical knowledge to the task of designing interesting, engaging, and satisfying human-computer activities. The effectiveness of these techniques relies on the relationship between form and experience, in terms of both the ways in which form influences content and the direct impact of the formal and structural qualities of a work on human thought and emotion.

### Drama Versus Narrative

One way to get at the special qualities of drama that are most relevant in the design of human-computer activity is to contrast it with a related form that has been more commonly employed by interface designers—namely, the art of narrative. Narrative has been employed as the structural backbone of such applications as adventure games and tutorial-style computer-assisted instruction. Its uses have also been investigated by workers in the area of information retrieval and presentation [see, for instance, Lehnert, 1977; Dyer, 1983; and Don, 1990].

Why have we chosen drama rather than narrative as a global model for human-computer activities? How are human-computer activities more like plays than stories? Can't we get the same kind of intellectual and emotional gratification from a good book as we do from a good play? To focus on the key differences, recall the basic Aristotelian definition of drama: the imitation of an action with a beginning, middle, and end, which is meant to be enacted in real time, as if the events were actually unfolding. Incidents are selected and arranged by the playwright in a way that is true to the causal relationships among them.

The key differences between drama and narrative can be summarized as follows:

- *Enactment*, meaning to act out rather than to read. Enacted representations involve direct sensing as well as cognition. To state it more simply, the stuff of narrative is *description*, while the stuff of drama is *action*.
- *Intensification*, meaning that incidents are selected, arranged, and represented, in general, so as to intensify emotion and condense time. Narrative forms generally employ the reverse process, *extensification*, where incidents may be reported from a number of perspectives and in ways that expand or explode time (for example, perceptions that take only an eye-blink in the "real time" of the characters in a novel by James Joyce or Virginia Woolf consume whole chapters with perceptual and cognitive detail). The common-sense observation is simply that time has a different scale when you are acting out than it does when you are reading. In Aristotelian terms, this is one of the *formal* differences between drama and narrative. (For a semioticist's view of the way in which drama accomplishes the condensation of action, see Hilton [1991], especially p. 4.)

- *Unity of action versus episodic structure:* Another basic difference between drama and narrative is in the structure of incidents. Dramas typically represent a strong central action with separate incidents that are causally linked to that action, something the neoclassicists called the *unity of action*. Narrative tends to be more episodic; that is, incidents are more likely to be quasi-independent and connected thematically rather than causally to the whole. Drama is typically more intense, tightly constructed, economical, and cathartic than narrative. And it is very important to remember that these things are part of the form itself; that is, *drama affords these qualities because of the kind of thing it is.*

The notion of enactment is intrinsic to human-computer activity because of its multisensory nature, as we discuss at length in this chapter and in Chapter 2. Another strong advantage of a dramatic model is illustrated by the simple observation that there are limits on the amount of time that a person can comfortably spend *actively* engaged in a representation. I know from many years of acting in and directing plays, and even from playing cowboys and Indians in my youth, that when you're *acting something out*, three or four hours is about the upper limit of your emotional energy. I know from the many hours that I spend humped up over a hot computer that the energy limit, at least for a person of my age range, is roughly the same.[1] Fundamentally, this is an issue of magnitude and closure. The criterion of magnitude (discussed near the end of Chapter 2) suggests that the limitation of *duration* of an action has aesthetic and cognitive aspects as well as physical ones.

---

[1]I feel obliged to include a remark by one of my anonymous reviewers: "Four hours max 'humped over a hot computer?' Wimp! In fact, I would argue that after four hours you may be just starting to get somewhere interesting . . ." My reply is, yes, I'm a wimp. Life is too short to beat the hell out of yourself doing something that should take a quarter of the time and be an order of magnitude more fun.

So, to return to the examples of a narrative approach to human-computer activity at the beginning of this section, we may observe that, in today's marketplace, narrative-style text adventure games have given way to graphical adventure games in which the action is represented in a multisensory, first-person way, with a stronger central action. The designers at Lucasfilm Games have been pioneers in this shift to a more dramatic approach. As Lucasfilm designer Ron Gilbert puts it:

> If I could have my way, I'd design games that were meant to be played in four to five hours. The games would be of the same scope that I currently design, I'd just remove the silly time-wasting puzzles and take the player for an intense ride. The experience they would leave with would be much more entertaining and a lot less frustrating. The games would still be challenging, but not at the expense of the player's patience [Gilbert, 1989].

Gilbert's philosophy has been evident in all of his recent game designs, and he and his colleagues at Lucasfilm should be credited with inventing an approach to adventure games that delivers all the punch of a good movie (see Color Plate I). Interestingly, although Lucasfilm's storytelling games do in fact take much less time to play than the average narrative-style adventure, people pay the same price for them—willingly trading off narrative duration and description for a shorter, more intense blast of dramatic excitement.

In the realm of computer-aided instruction, dramatic and simulation-based approaches have largely supplanted tutorials in many content domains.[2] Among the leaders in this trend has been Joyce Hakansson, who has designed and produced such learning products as *Ducks Ahoy!*, in which adventures with ducks in Venice help young students gain

---

[2]In 1981, I attended a meeting of the National Council of Teachers of Mathematics. In those days, teachers preferred computer programs that provided drill and practice, and they were extremely skeptical of "game-like" approaches. There were, however, several highly successful game-like activities that were being used in classrooms. A survey of teachers revealed that when a learning game was effective in the classroom, it was reclassified by teachers as a "simulation," thus circumventing the categorical problem with games.

dynamic planning skills, and *Seahorse Hide 'n' Seek,* through which children develop sensitivity to color, shape, and scale by helping a seahorse hide from its predators in an underwater landscape. The product has also been used as a beginning point for creative improvisations among its young users. Another pioneering group is The Learning Company, publisher of such products as *Rocky's Boots* and *Reader Rabbit,* in which basic concepts in science and language arts are learned through the manipulation of virtual objects in dramatic contexts.[3] In the realm of information retrieval and multimedia design, the Guides project described in Chapter 6 will be used as an example of an approach that involves both narrative and dramatic elements. Finally, the new computer-based medium known as virtual reality (also discussed in Chapter 6) employs a fundamentally dramatic approach to applications such as training simulation and scientific visualization.

## Structure and Artistry

For the nonspecialist, the idea of a dramatic model may seem to have more to do with content—interesting situations and colorful characters, for instance—than with structure. As a structuralist critic, I have been assailed by both theatre and computer people for taking what they perceive as a rather bloodless approach. Structure is not always well understood, and even when it is, its uses are seen to be analytical rather than productive. When we see a good film or go to a good play, we are moved by things that seem to transcend structuralism—a beautiful image, dialogue and action that speak deeply and genuinely about life. There seems to be a contradiction here. If it's all so structured, how does it get to seem so lifelike? Surely there is more to it than structure, more to it than a computer could be programmed to create. People

[3]It is interesting to note that the designer of *Rocky's Boots,* a landmark simulation that helps kids learn about logic by constructing circuits and using them to create more elaborate systems, was also the creator of the first graphic adventure game, *Adventure,* implemented for the Atari VCS in 1979. Warren Robinett is now a leading programmer in the virtual-reality medium. All of his work illustrates a dramatic notion of enactment.

often criticize my approach by countering that a computer program can never be smart or sensitive enough to make a beautiful work of art.

These observations are, I think, absolutely true, and they point to the artistry that is essential in every beautiful made thing. Artistry transcends and saturates the process. We do not know what it is that gives a person the ability to conceive or create magnificence in art. We cannot hope to recreate such ability computationally, at least not with today's technology or any of its conceivable descendants. But our discussion of the structural aspects of a "beautiful" dramatic action is not intended to serve as a wholly sufficient explanation for its beauty. Human-computer activity, like other art forms, requires artistry that can be contributed only by human beings. But artistry is deployed within the constraints of the medium, the tools, and the formal and structural characteristics of the kind of thing that the artist is trying to create. Artistry and structure are interdependent; both must be present if beauty is to be the result. Perhaps more important in this stage of the evolution of computer-based media is the fact that artistic sensibility must drive the notion of *desired experience* from which the design of technological components must be derived.

Human-computer activity is like drama in the sense that the primary designer (or playwright) is not the only human source of artistry in the completed whole. In the case of theatre, the director, actors, designers, and technicians who are involved in rendering a performance all make contributions that require artistry. In human-computer activity, there may be a legion of programmers who have designed and architected programs on which a given activity depends, graphic designers who created images and animation, wordsmiths who authored text (or text-generating algorithms), and so on. A fundamental but often overlooked source of human artistry is the people who actually engage in the designed activity; that is, the *human agents*. (The notion of human agency—the active collaboration of people with programs in the shaping of human-computer experiences—is the reason for my avoidance of the word "user" throughout this book.)

# *Constraints*

Everyone who participates in an artistic endeavor, be they playwrights, actors, visual artists, or human agents, exercises creativity. One of the less known contributions of structure is its role in *constraining* the creative process. The relationship between creativity and constraints is mysterious and symbiotic.

Constraints—limitations on human behavior—may be expressed as anything from gentle suggestions to stringent rules, or they may be only subconsciously sensed as intrinsic aspects of the thing that a person is trying to do or be or create. All of us are always operating under some set of constraints: the physical requirements of survival (the need for air, food, and water); the limitations of language on verbal expression; the rules of social acceptability in public situations (e.g., wearing clothes). The ability to act without any such constraints is the stuff of fantasy—the dream of flight, for instance, or the pursuit of immortality. Yet even such fantasy powers can be lost by the failure to comply with other, albeit mythical, constraints (witness Prometheus). It is difficult to imagine life, even a fantasy life, in the absence of any constraints at all.

## Why People Must Be Constrained

People engaged in human-computer activities are subject to some special kinds of constraints. Some constraints arise from the technical capabilities and limitations of the system itself: If the system has no speech processing capability, for instance, a person must employ the keyboard for verbal input and is constrained by its vicissitudes—the "QWERTY" layout, for example, and the presence or absence of function keys. Other constraints arise from the nature of the activity as it is comprehended by the system. Typically, what you can do in a given application environment such as a word processor, drawing program, or computer game is but a subset of all that you might be able to do with your computer.

The design of a human-computer activity should be informed by an analysis of constraints to determine how much people should be constrained and what kinds of constraints are most appropriate. That analysis begins with understanding the various reasons why constraints are necessary.

The hardware-related reasons for constraints are fairly straightforward. They will also change, depending upon the elaborateness, completeness, and cost of various implementations of the system. For example, pointing devices that can be used to enable gestural input currently have a limited range; hence people must be constrained to stand within a few feet of a receiver.[4] Physical acts like running or manipulating objects in a fantasy world require that conventions be devised through which the desire to perform such actions can be expressed. Such conventions, mandated by the technical limitations of systems, are a form of constraints.

Constraints are necessary to contain the action within the mimetic world—a software-related problem. For example, in an interactive fantasy version of a Sherlock Holmes mystery, it would be important to constrain people to the customs and technology of Arthur Conan Doyle's nineteenth-century London (for example, no ballistics tests could be used to prove that a bullet was fired by a certain gun). Any human-computer system, no matter how elaborate, cannot be expected to comprehend all possible worlds simultaneously. Preventing people from introducing new potential is essential in the creation and maintenance of dramatic probability.

What is the relationship between the experience of creativity and the constraints under which we perform creative acts? In fantasies about human-computer systems, people like computer-game enthusiasts and science-fiction writers tend to imagine magical spaces where they can invent their own worlds and do whatever they wish—like gods [for example, see Vinge, 1981]. Even if such a system were technically feasible—which it is not, at the moment (the rhetoric of virtual

---

[4]Recently, I took part in a demonstration of a new CD-I player that employed an infrared remote controller. I pointed at the screen, pressed the button, and nothing happened. The demonstrator hastily explained that the pointing device was, of course, "talking to" the console that was placed a few feet to the left of the screen and not to the screen itself—a constraint that threatened to short-circuit my nervous system.

## Color Plate I

**Ron Gilbert's *The Secret of Monkey Island*.** The game takes players for an intense, first-person romp through a pirate's world.

Graphics by Steve Purcell, Mike Ebert, Mark Ferrari, and Martin Cameron. 

## Color Plate II

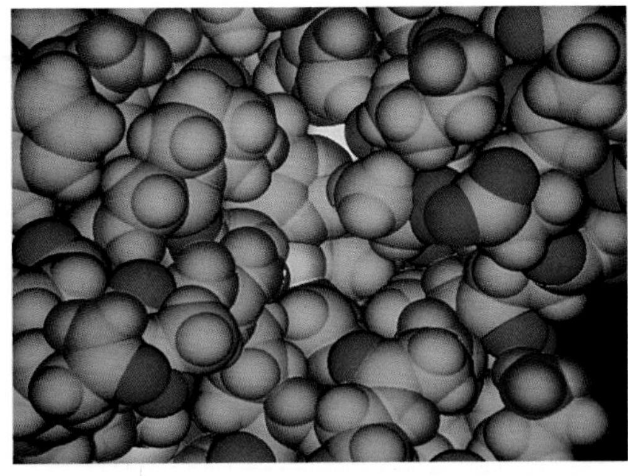

**Docking molecules at the University of North Carolina's Virtual Reality Laboratory.** The multisensory representation allows a person to employ physical as well as intellectual skills in solving such problems.

Courtesy of GRIP Project, Department of Computer Science, University of North Carolina at Chapel Hill. Supported by the National Institutes of Health, Division of Research Resources, under grant RR-02170.

## Color Plate IV

**A character from *Hidden Agenda* by TRANSFiction Systems.** Characters change their behaviors in response to the player's choices and actions as the leader of a Central American country.

## Color Plate III

**Autodesk's three-dimensional CAD program.** The system allows direct manipulation of scale and allows for better visualization through the ability to fluidly change visual and conceptual point of view.

(a) The Orlando International AutoCAD computer-aided design (CAD) software from Autodesk. This shaded visualization shows the main elements of the project.

(b) This shaded rendering demonstrates the capability of AutoShade to enhance the model geometry created in AutoCAD. Shown are the skylight and supporting structure in the airside building's transfer section.

Used with permission.

## Color Plate V

**Screens from *Habitat*, a networked world developed by Lucasfilm Games in association with Quantum Computer Services, Inc.**



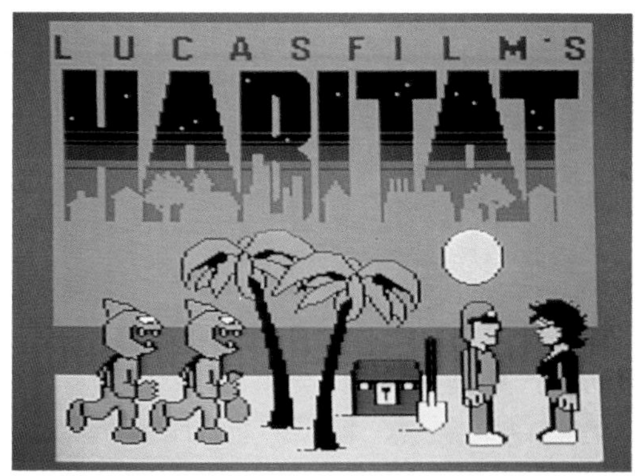

## Color Plate VI

**The custom guides workshop in Guides 3.0.** The System Guide is available to coach people on the use of the workshop. The window at the right of the display gives a dynamic "preview" of the information items that a custom guide prefers based on the topics a person has told it to be interested in.

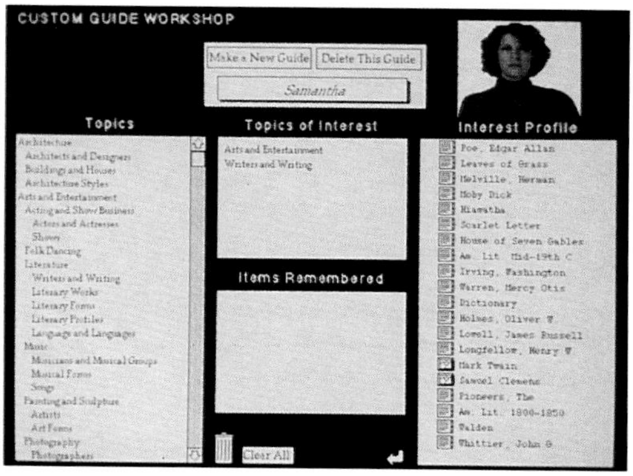

## Color Plate VII

**Lively agents help people find information in the Guides project.**



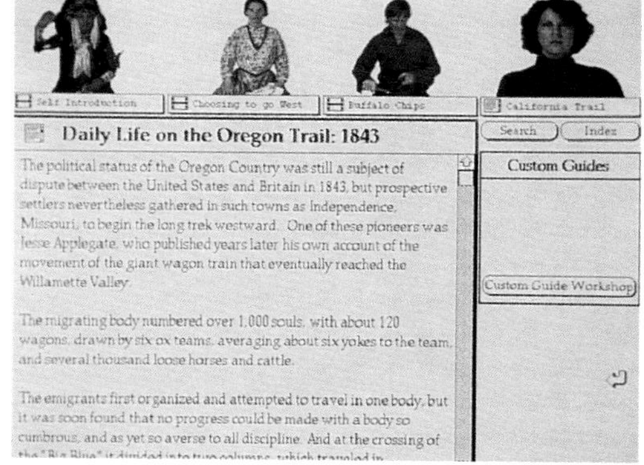


## Color Plate VIII

**The NewSpeek display developed by Walter Bender.**

Reuters Ltd June 17, 1986, Tuesday, AM cycle
BURGER RESIGNS FROM SUPREME COURT, REAGAN NAMES REHNQUIST
By Patricia Wilson
Chief Justice Warren Burger resigned from the Supreme Court today and President Reagan named Associate Justice William Rehnquist, the most conservative of the nine justices, to succeed him. Reagan also nominated another conservative jurist, Antonin Scalia, a 50-year-old federal appeals court judge, to fill Rehnquist's seat.

## Color Plate IX

**The "old" and "new" settler woman guide.** The new version is shot against a neutral background, and the costume has been toned down to merely suggest the character's historical role.

## Color Plate X

**Scenes of a virtual reality office that users may "enter," created by the Cyberspace Research team at Autodesk, Inc.** Interactivity in Cyberspace includes such actions as grasping, moving, releasing, throwing, etc.

Used with permission.

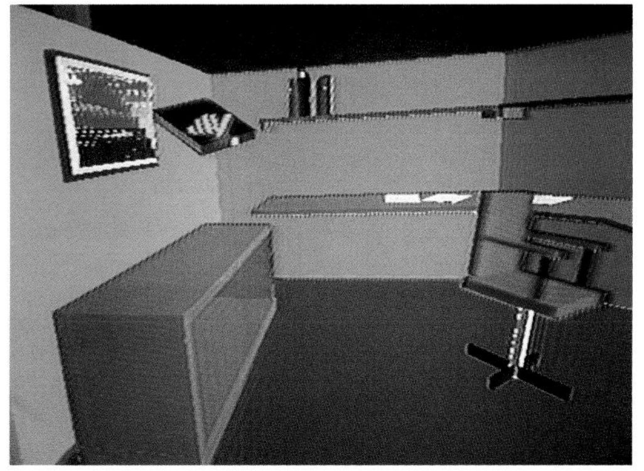

## Color Plate XI

**The Holodeck, today's cultural icon for the promise of dramatic human-computer activity.** In this episode, two members of the Starship Enterprise crew relax with an interactive Sherlock Holmes mystery.

**Color Plate XII**
**Anasazi petroglyphs.**
Photograph by Kurt Hulteen.

**Color Plate XIII**
**The great kiva at Chaco Canyon.**
Photograph by Kurt Hulteen.

reality notwithstanding)—the experience of using it might be more like an existential nightmare than a dream of freedom.

The relationship between creativity and limitations has been examined in some depth by psychologist Rollo May. In *The Courage to Create,* May asserts the need for limitations in creative activities:

> Creativity arises out of the tension between spontaneity and limitations, the latter (like river banks) forcing the spontaneity into the various forms which are essential to the work of art. . . . The significance of limits in art is seen most clearly when we consider the question of form. Form provides the essential boundaries and structure for the creative act [May, 1975].

A system in which people are encouraged to do whatever they want will probably not produce pleasant experiences. When a person is asked to "be creative" with no direction or constraints whatever, the result is, according to May, often a sense of powerlessness or even complete paralysis of the imagination. Limitations—constraints that focus creative efforts—paradoxically increase our imaginative power by reducing the number of possibilities open to us. Limitations provide the security net that enables us to take imaginative leaps:

> Imagination is casting off mooring ropes, taking one's chances that there will be new mooring posts in the vastness ahead. . . . How far can we let our imagination loose? . . . Will we lose the boundaries that enable us to orient ourselves to what we call reality? This again is the problem of form, or stated differently, the awareness of limits [May, 1975].

The closed, knowable nature of a mimetic world provides a similar security net. People respect the limits of a mimetic world by refraining from introducing new potential into it (for instance, avoiding words or actions that the system is unlikely to "know" about). In exchange for this complicity, people experience increased potential for effective agency, in worlds in which the causal relations among events are not obscured by the randomness and noise characteristic of open systems (like "real life").

## Characteristics of Good Constraints

May's analysis suggests that constraints—limitations on the scope and nature of invention—are essential to creativity. Certainly, some constraints on the choices and actions that may be expressed by people are technically essential to any human-computer activity. The question is how those constraints should be determined and expressed. The standard techniques for introducing constraints—instructions, error messages, or dialogue boxes, for instance—are almost always destructive of our *engagement* in the activity by forcing us to "pop out" of the mimetic context into a metacontext of interface operations.

Constraints can be either *explicit* or *implicit*. Explicit constraints, as in the case of menus or command languages, are undisguised and directly available. When we are in doubt about the "legality" of certain choices or actions, we should be able to find the rules and protocols of a system straightforwardly expressed, either in the manual, or in an on-line "help" facility. Implicit constraints, on the other hand, may be inferred from the behavior of the system. We can identify implicit constraints when a system fails to allow us to make certain kinds of choices. There is no way, for example, to negotiate with the enemy in most combat-based computer action games. In most word processors, there is no facility for "drawing" or "painting" images in a document, and the absence of drawing tools makes it less likely that we will think of doing so. Some constraints have both implicit and explicit qualities. In Microsoft Excel, for example, menu-based operations are not selectable and the document cannot be closed until the current item has been properly entered on the spreadsheet. If we attempt such an "illegal" maneuver, nothing happens at all. We may infer from this "nonbehavior" that we must do something else or do something differently.

Explicit constraints can be used without damage to engagement if they are presented before the action begins. A good example is the determination and expression of rules in child's play, which occurs before play actually begins and creates a contract binding the participants to behave within certain constraints. Once the action has started, however, explicit constraints often prove disruptive—an argument about the rules can ruin a perfectly good session of cowboys and Indians ("Wait a minute—who says Indians can only be killed with silver bullets?").[5] Implicit constraints are preferable during the course of the action, simply because the means for expressing them are usually less intrusive than those used for explicit constraints.

Constraints may also be characterized as *extrinsic* or *intrinsic* to the mimetic action. Extrinsic constraints have to do, not with the mimetic context, but with the context of the person as operator of the system. Avoiding the "reset" and "escape" keys during play of a game has nothing to do with the game world and everything to do with the behavior of the computer. Playing an improvised scene without the use of language has nothing to do with the dramatic action of the scene but is an extrinsic constraint designed to improve the actors' gestural acuity—a different context than the mimetic one. Extrinsic constraints have been used successfully in a variety of sports and other disciplines to distract the part of consciousness that can interfere with performance [see Gallwey, 1976]. The technique is generally inappropriate in human-computer activity, however, because it sets up a secondary context that demands part of a person's attention.

Extrinsic constraints can be made to appear intrinsic when they are expressed in terms of the mimetic context. If the "escape" key is defined as a self-destruct mechanism, for

---

[5]An interesting exception is the ongoing process of rule-making and enforcement that is sometimes an element in children's play—a sort of *metagame* that provides its own distinct pleasures. A similar metagame occurs in the theatre when stagehands and "real people" wander in and out of the action, as in some of the plays of Christopher Durang and Thornton Wilder, or in certain productions of Brecht. Seen in this way, the metagame is also mimetic, and the actors are merely performing the roles of "real people" as well as portraying other dramatic characters. Because it is mimetic, this is a "false" context shift, much like a play within a play, or a dream in which one has false awakenings. Such metagames or metaplays do not violate engagement, but enhance it through the same means as the mimetic "core" activity.

instance, the constraint against pressing it in the course of flying a mimetic spaceship is intrinsic to the action. We need not shift gears to consider the effect of the key upon the computer or the game program. Expressing constraints in this manner preserves the contextual aspect of engagement.

Another good example of well-contextualized extrinsic constraints is the "borders" option in Microsoft Word 4.0. Once we have reached the screen in which borders can be created, we see a graphical, direct-manipulation interface. We can move lines of various types around in a representation of a document until the desired border style has been achieved. Unfortunately, getting to this neat little border construction screen is problematic at best. We must select "paragraph" from the "format" menu and then click on a "borders" button on the paragraph screen, a logical hierarchy that is forced upon the activity. Directness is obliterated by the operational overhead created by this scheme. A second problem is that buttons defining border styles coexist with the direct-manipulation display on the borders screen and have doppelgänger functionality. Nested within the button problem is the additional difficulty that the top three buttons invoke actions, while the fourth is also used inconsistently to indicate a state or mode that we may have entered by combining other elements via direct manipulation. No wonder people have difficulty with it. (My husband, a senior engineer at Apple Computer, hasn't figured it out.)

The mimetic context itself can be teased apart, especially in task-oriented activities. Bødker [1989] uses the interface for creating footnotes in Microsoft Word as an example of how a task that is part of the general context of document creation is nevertheless extrinsic to the subcontext of writing the text. The WYSIWYG-style interface for authoring does not work for footnote creation; the flow of the authoring activity is disrupted by the dialogue box that requires the author to specify the form of a footnote before actually writing it. The point here is that an activity that may be part of the mimetic whole can be seen to inject extrinsic constraints if it is staged or represented poorly. Bødker's example can be seen as a failure in the arrangement of incidents, with the by-product of disrupting engagement.

Constraints should be applied without shrinking our perceived range of freedom of action: Constraints should limit, not what we can do, but what we are likely to think of doing. Such *implicit* constraints, when successful, eliminate the need for explicit limitations on our behavior. Context is the most effective medium for establishing implicit constraints. The ability to recognize and comply with implicit, context-based constraints is a common human skill, exercised automatically in most situations and not requiring concentrated effort or explicit attention. It is the same skill that we use to determine what to say and how to act when we interact with a group of unfamiliar people—at a party, for instance. The limitations on behavior are not likely to be explicitly known or consciously mulled over; they arise naturally from our growing knowledge of the context. The situational aspects of the current context and the way in which they have evolved over the course of the action establish dramatic probability that influences our actions and expectations. In summary, then, constraints that are implicit and intrinsic to the mimetic context are least destructive of engagement and other qualities of experience, although explicit and extrinsic constraints can be successfully employed if they frame rather than intrude upon the action.

## Establishing Constraints Through Character and Action

Since human-computer activities are dramatic in nature, it is reasonable to look for guidance in the development of constraints to other dramatic forms: theatrical performance and improvisation. In the theatre, the actor is constrained in the performance of a character primarily by the script, and secondarily by the director, the accoutrements of the theatre (including scenic elements, properties, and costumes), and the performances of fellow actors. The actor must work within exacting constraints, which dictate the character's every word, choice, and action. In spite of these narrow limits, the actor still has ample latitude for individual creativity. In the words of acting teacher Michael Chekhov:

> Every role offers an actor the opportunity to improvise, to collaborate and truly co-create with the author and director. This suggestion, of course, does not imply improvising new lines or substituting business for that outlined by the director. On the contrary. The given lines and the business are the firm bases upon which the actor must and can develop his improvisations. *How* he speaks the lines and *how* he fulfills the business are the open gates to a vast field of improvisation. The "hows" of his lines and business are the ways in which he can express himself freely [Chekhov, 1953].

The value of limitations in focusing creative activity is recognized in the theory and practice of theatrical improvisation. Constraints on the choices and actions of actors improvising characters are probably most explicit in the tradition of *commedia dell'arte*. Stock characters and fixed scenarios provide *formal* constraints on the action in that they affect the actor's choices through formal causality. Conventionalized costumes for each character, a standard collection of scenic elements and properties, and a repertoire of *lazzi* (standard bits of business) provide *material* constraints on the action. Likewise, people who are engaged in computer-based mimetic activities are subject to formal and material constraints.

Constraints expressed on the level of character may function as either material or formal constraints, depending upon how they affect the action. Traits and predispositions provide materials from which action is formulated. They also give form to thought, language, and enactment.

Specific objectives or motivations on the part of the human agent(s) constrain the action in both games and task-oriented applications. Highest-level objectives (or, in the lingo of method acting, "super-objectives") are usually known explicitly before the action begins. Computer games provide obvious examples. In *Star Raiders*, for instance, the objective of the human character is to destroy all the Zylons in several quadrants of the galaxy. In *Zork*, the objective is to gather all the treasures in the maze and return them to the trophy room. In

Parker Brothers' *The Empire Strikes Back*, the objective is to destroy as many of the Imperial Walkers as possible before they reach the power plant and blow up the planet. However, as science fiction author Harlan Ellison observed in an unpublished review of the game, it is not possible to meet that goal because the bad guys just keep getting better—an affliction shared by many video games. "The lesson," moans Ellison, "is the lesson of Sisyphus. You cannot win. You can only waste your life struggling and struggling, getting as good as you can be, with no hope of triumph." One might speculate that this incredibly frustrating feature of game design contributed to the decline of the video-game genre in 1983 and 1984.

In task-oriented applications, the choice of the application itself indicates an awareness of super-objectives: Word processors are used to create documents, drawing programs are used to create graphical compositions, etc. However, as applications become more integrated and flexible (or are replaced by "environments" as conceptual units in the human-computer universe), people's goals cannot be so readily inferred by simply noticing what applications they launch. Increasingly, systems will need to employ either explicit conversations with people to determine task objectives or implicit user-modeling techniques to infer objectives from behavior, as discussed below.

The way in which a computer-based system responds to a person can help to narrow down and flesh out the person's objectives, and it can also lead to fairly predictable kinds of action. People who play computer games find that their objectives are rapidly elaborated as the action progresses, through the workings of dramatic probability. As the Zylons close in on a friendly starbase in a game of *Star Raiders*, for instance, we discover that we must develop a strategy for preventing the starbase from being surrounded or captured in order to fulfill our super-objective; otherwise, the action will be prematurely terminated. Hence a whole series of fairly predictable, causally related choices on the part of the human character is stimulated by the single super-objective that has been expressed as a formal constraint at the beginning of the game.

When a person's super-objective is not clear-cut from the point of view of the computer (as in the case of integrated applications or environments), techniques could be devised for inferring it, without imposing explicit limitations. For instance, the system might notice what tools we select, how often, and in what combinations. This noticing behavior could enable the formulation of a hypothesis about our immediate objective, leading to the automatic tailoring of the environment and tools. As other tool sets are used, the system could formulate a more global hypothesis about the whole activity. If the activity is such that inferences of this type have a low probability of being accurate or a high probability of being annoying or confusing, explicit dialogue could be employed. Explicit dialogues with the "system" about our intentions (as in the Bødker example earlier in this chapter) can be tedious and disruptive. Conversely, casting the conversational partner as an agent *character* (as opposed to the amorphous "system") can provide contextual smoothing. For instance, in a research project at Apple Computer, Allen Cypher developed a program that can sense repetitive activity (Figure 4.1). When the program notices that a person is doing something over and over (such as adding numbers or animating an object frame-by-frame), an agent named "Eager" appears and offers up a plan for completing the activity. This highly animated dialogue, coupled with the program's power to clarify the person's objectives and help to achieve them, provides a very attractive means for introducing formal constraints [Cypher, 1990 and 1991].

In activities where we interact with more contentful worlds (such as simulation environments), a system might utilize templates to ascertain our objectives. A system could notice what we are doing, select a template that most nearly matches our apparent motivation, and adjust the system's contributions to the action accordingly. For instance, a person interacting with a simulation of a space station might be trying to redesign it or trying to learn how to operate its controls, or perhaps to experience the environment under various conditions. There is the beginning of a "plot" implicit in each of these goals, and the system could assist in bringing that plot to life. The system's reasoning might go something like this: "If he is doing *x*, then he probably wants *y*. Therefore incidents *a*, *b*, and *c* are likely to cause him to make choices *d*, *e*, and *f*." A template would contain the candidate objective and a set of incidents that would be likely to elicit certain responses based on that objective. The system might then use the person's actual responses as a measure of the accuracy of its initial inference and switch templates if necessary. When it had established a person's objective with a high degree of confidence, the system might kick off a specific scenario by enacting a predesigned *inciting incident*. Furthermore, information about individual people could augment such templates, tailoring the action to such traits as a person's job and skills as well. Such templates would function as recipes for the formulation of action and could be used to both predict and constrain a person's behavior.

Material constraints may be provided implicitly through exposition presented during the action. People discover "physical" and behavioral aspects of a mimetic world, characters, and past events in this manner. To ensure that people become familiar with such elements early on, the designer of a simulation-based activity may wish to delay active human participation until the bulk of the exposition has been presented. The "attract mode" of many arcade games performs this expository function. The notion of "guided tours" employed by Apple Computer attempts to exhibit the properties and behaviors of key objects in narrated simulations, a kind of preactivity exposition. In the Guides project at Apple, the represented character actions of slumping, doing other things, and falling asleep indicate through enactment a guide's reduced level of interest in the piece of information that is currently displayed. This expository behavior implies that the guide will have little to suggest in the way of related items.

The kinds of actions that a person can take in representational worlds are also constrained by the capabilities of the input and output devices used in the system. By constraining what—or whether—people may see, hear, and say, the system

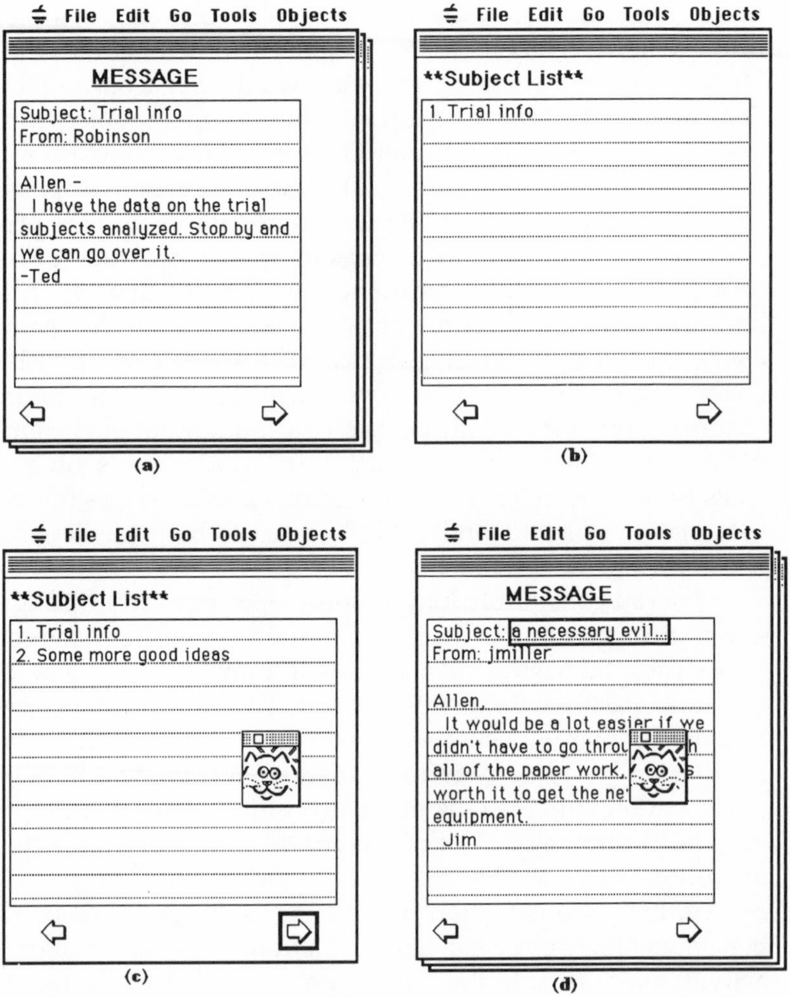

*Figure 4.1* "Eager" is an agent-like entity that notices patterns of action and tries to create programs to continue those patterns. Here, the user has a stack of message cards (a) and she wants to make a list of the subjects of the messages. She copies the first subject and pastes it into a new "Subject List" card (b). Then she goes to the second message, copies its subject, and adds it to the list. At this point, the Eager icon pops up (c), since Eager has detected a pattern in the user's actions. Eager also highlights the right-arrow

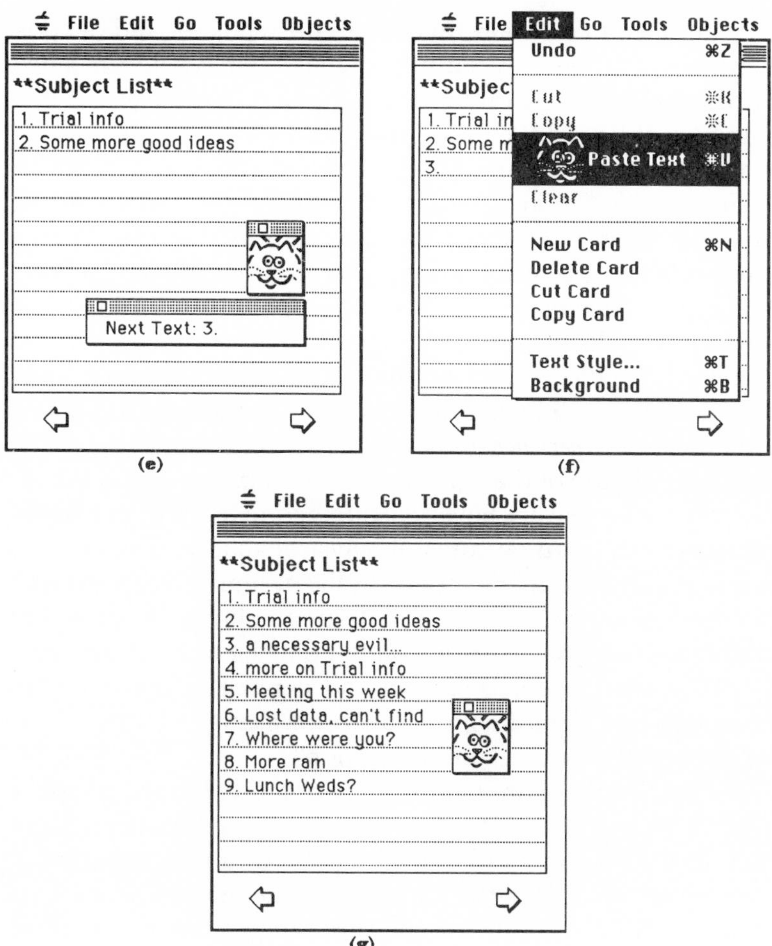


(e)

(f)

(g)

button in green (c), since it anticipates that the user will click here next. Eager continues anticipating that the user will navigate to the third message, select (d) and copy its subject, go to the Subject List, click at the start of the third line (e), type "3" (f), and then paste in the subject (g). The user is now confident that Eager knows what to do, so she clicks on the Eager icon and it completes the task automatically (h).

may implicitly constrain their thoughts, choices, and actions. In systems that employ simple language parsers, for instance, words that are unknown to the system cannot effect any change in the world; choices and actions that are represented by unknown words cannot be performed.

It is difficult to avoid such a disruptive effect when people are allowed or encouraged to make choices that they cannot effectively express to the system. For instance, the text adventure games developed by Infocom are presented entirely in a verbal mode. People are encouraged to use natural language to express their choices, and so they expect words to work. They have no clue to tell them which words are unknown to the system *except the experience of failure*. On the other hand, given the text-based nature of the game and the equipment that it is usually run on, people are never encouraged to attempt to express themselves through gestures or physical actions. The absence of visual and kinesthetic modes in the system is accepted as a given, and the resulting constraints are unobtrusive. Such constraints are extrinsic to the action but may be utilized effectively if they are presented simply and explicitly, or if they are integrated into the mimetic context (for example, "this ship is not equipped for voice communication").

Generally, the more modes that are present in the interface (verbal, visual, auditory, etc.), the more complex the system must be in order to handle the reception and interpretation of a wide variety of inputs and to formulate and orchestrate its responses. Constraining people through limitations on input and output capabilities becomes less effective as the number of modes in the interface increases; separate sets of constraints for each mode serve to confuse and frustrate people. In a multimodal interface environment, intrinsic formal and material constraints are therefore preferable to those based on the technical characteristics of the interface.

## Engagement: The First-Person Imperative

In the foregoing discussion, *engagement* was held up as a desirable—even essential—human response to computer-mediated activities. Engagement has cognitive components, but it is primarily understood as an emotion. Why should we demand that all human-computer activities elicit this particular emotional response? What is its nature, and what is its value? What can designers do to guarantee that it occurs?

Engagement, as I use the concept in this book, is similar in many ways to the theatrical notion of the "willing suspension of disbelief," a concept introduced by the early nineteenth-century critic and poet Samuel Taylor Coleridge.[6] It is the state of mind that we must attain in order to enjoy a representation of an action. Coleridge believed that any idiot could see that a play on a stage was not real life. (Plato would have disagreed with him, as do those in whom fear is induced by any new representational medium, but that is another story.) Coleridge noticed that, in order to enjoy a play, we must temporarily suspend (or attenuate) our knowledge that it is "pretend." We do this "willingly" in order to experience other emotional responses as a result of viewing the action. When the heroine is threatened, we feel a kind of fear for and with her that is recognizable as fear but different from the fear we would feel if we were tied to the railroad tracks ourselves. *Pretending that the action is real* affords us the thrill of fear; *knowing that the action is pretend* saves us from the pain of fear. Furthermore, our fear is flavored by the delicious expectation that the young lady will be saved in a heroic manner—an emotional response that derives from knowledge about the *form* of melodrama.

The phenomenon that Coleridge described can be seen to occur almost identically in drama and computer games, where we feel for and with the characters (including *ourselves* as characters) in very similar ways. Yes, someone might cry, but manuscripts and spreadsheets aren't pretend! Here we must separate the activity from its artifacts. The *representation* of a manuscript or spreadsheet as we manipulate it on the screen is in fact pretend, as compared to physical artifacts like data files (in the computer's memory or on a storage medium) and hard copy. The artifacts are real (as are actors, lighting

---

[6]For an analysis and thorough bibliography of Coleridge's criticism, see Allen and Clark [1962], pp. 221–239.

instruments, and reels of motion-picture film), but the rules involved in working with the *representations* (plays or human-computer activities) must subsume the knowledge, at some level, that they are representations. Why? First, because the fact that they are representations is the key to understanding what we can do with them. Second, because their special status as representations affects our emotions about them, enabling experiences that are, in the main, much more pleasurable than those we feel in real life. The distinguishing characteristic of the emotions we feel in a representational context is that there is *no threat of pain or harm in the real world*.

The key to applying the notion of "willing suspension of disbelief" to representational activities that have real-world artifacts is to ensure that the likelihood of *unintentional* effects on those artifacts approaches zero. The other day I experienced a power failure while I was working on this manuscript. I had learned to save my work often, but losing just a few paragraphs evoked plenty of unpleasant real-world emotion. Quite simply, *my system should never have let that happen*. My first word processor, although it lacked nearly all of the features that I appreciate in the one I use today, had a fail-safe feature that took the opportunity to automatically save an active file whenever there was a pause in the input stream—on the average, about every seven seconds. For people who use systems without such a feature, a power outage can be a context shift of the worst possible kind. Such interruptions to the flow of representational activity must be avoided if the powers of representational media are to be preserved. Saving my work has receded from an obsession to a kind of tic, but it shouldn't be there nipping at my subconscious at all.

Furthermore, engagement entails a kind of playfulness—the ability to fool around, to spin out "what if" scenarios. Such "playful" behavior is easy to see in the way that people use spreadsheets and word processors. In my house-buying example in the previous chapter, I played around with different scenarios for making trade-offs in my purchase decision. The key quality that a system must possess in order to foster this kind of engagement is reversibility—that is, the ability to take something back. What if I failed to save a copy of my spreadsheet before I monkeyed around with a scenario that turned out to be disastrous? What if that scenario altered a significant amount of my data? The theory of hypertext suggests one solution, where various stages of a "document" (or, more correctly, an activity) can be saved and linked to the current version. This solution is unsatisfactory in that it is likely (at least in contemporary hypertext systems) to create a bewildering proliferation of documents. I don't really want to page back through versions of my work; I want to turn back the clock. The dimension of change is best represented through time, not fixed states. A simple chrono-scrollbar would suffice. Yes, the implementation is hard, but the hardest part is probably visualizing the appropriate representation in the first place.

I notice how word processing has changed my writing style. Now I am able to move chunks of text (roughly corresponding to ideas or elements in an argument) around within a document. I can more easily experiment with the visual components of the information I am creating by changing fonts and paragraph styles. But there is nothing sadder or more disruptive than seeing the message, `"Can't Undo."` With a typewriter, I still had the hard copy and a handy bottle of correcting fluid. Here again, the notion of document creation as an activity unfolding through time is superior to a notion of independent operations on an artifact of which one must remember to take snapshots.

Engagement is what happens when we are able to give ourselves over to a representational action, comfortably and unambiguously. It involves a kind of complicity. We agree to think and feel in terms of both the content and conventions of a mimetic context. In return, we gain a plethora of new possibilities for action and a kind of emotional guarantee. One reason why people are amenable to constraints is the desire to gain these benefits.

Engagement is only possible when we can rely on the system to maintain the representational context. A person should never be forced to interact with the system *qua* system; indeed, any awareness of the system as a distinct, "real" entity would explode the mimetic illusion, just as a clear view of the stage manager calling cues would disrupt the "willing suspension of disbelief" for the audience of a traditional play. Engagement means that a person can experience a mimetic world directly, without mediation or distraction. Harking back to the slogan, "the representation is all there is," we can see that interface designers are often engaged in the wrong activity—that is, representing what the *computer* is doing. The proper object of an "interface" representation is what the *person* is doing with the computer—the action. Thinking about things this way automatically avoids the trapdoors into meta-level transactions with "the system."

## Characteristics of First-Person Experience

Another way to describe a person's involvement in the representational context of human-computer activity is as a *first-person* experience [see Laurel, 1986b]. In grammar, the personness of pronouns reflects where one stands *in relation to* others and the world. Most movies and novels, for example, are third-person experiences; the viewer or reader is "outside" the action and would describe what goes on using third-person pronouns: "First he did this, then they did that." Most instructional documents are second-person affairs: "Insert Tab A into Slot B"; "Honor your father and your mother." Operating a computer program is all too often a second-person experience: A person makes imperative statements (or pleas) to the system, and the *system* takes action, completely usurping the role of agency.

*Agency* is a key component of first-person experience. Although we may describe experiences in which we are not an agent using first-person pronouns (I saw this, I smelled that), the ability to *do* something sooner or later emerges as a criterion. On the one hand, doing very simple things can be an expression of agency—looking around, for instance, or reaching out and touching something (such simple types of agency are often responsible for the "breakthrough" experiences reported by many people who have used contemporary virtual-reality systems). On the other hand, doing something relatively complex in an indirect or mediated way may not have a first-person feel. In the early days of computing, programmers would submit a program and data on punched cards and come back to pick up the results a day or two later. Although they were telling the computer what to do quite exactly, during the hours of waiting for the computer to "crunch" those programmers were not experiencing a feeling of agency. Today, imploring a system to do something in a highly constrained, formal language can engender a similar feeling that somebody (or something) else is in control.

This is not to say that people cannot experience agency when there are computer-based agents in the representational environment. Agents that are well characterized and amenable to dialogue and collaboration can give a person the sense of being one of several agents in a complex action. An agent can be a mentor or a dictator, a liberator or a jailor. The difference is in the person's experience of *agency*—the power to take action—whether the context includes other agents or not.

First-person sensory qualities are as important as the sense of agency in creating satisfying human-computer experiences. Quite simply, the experience of first-person participation tends to be related to the number, variety, and integration of sensory modalities involved in the representation. The underlying principle here is *mimetic*; that is, a human-computer experience is more nearly "first-person" when the activity it represents unfolds in the appropriate sensory modalities. The intuitive correctness of this notion is witnessed by the direction of technical evolution in the areas of simulators and games—toward higher resolution graphics and faster animation, greater sound capabilities, motion platforms, and mimetic input devices like force-feedback controllers. In task-oriented applications, new technologies are allowing researchers to replace indirect or symbolic representations and manipulations with direct, concrete ones—for example, physically pointing or speaking as opposed to typing, spatial and graphical representation of data as opposed to textual representation, etc. (see Color Plates II and III). Likewise, the evolution of natural-language interfaces is beginning to replace the elaborate conventions of menu-based and command-based systems with systems that employ language in ways that are mimetic of real-world activities like conversation and question-and-answer dialogues [see, for instance, Schmandt, 1985].[7]

Sensory first-personness is not limited to the system's "output"; it must include the modalities that people can employ when they take action in mimetic worlds. Since it is all one representation, the desire for symmetry between "input" and "output" modalities is strong. Engagement is disrupted when my machine talks to me (especially if it asks me a question) and I can't *talk* back.[8] Furthermore, the real-world relationships among modalities affect our expectations in representational worlds that include them; for instance, greater force applied to the throwing of an object should make it appear to go farther, surfaces that look bumpy should feel bumpy, and balloons make noise when they pop.

When we sit back and contemplate the complexity involved in creating first-person experiences, we are tempted to see them as a luxury, not a necessity. But we mustn't fall prey to the notion that more is always better, or that our task is the seemingly impossible one of emulating the sensory and experiential bandwidth of the real world. Artistic selectivity is the countervailing force—capturing what is essential in the most effective and economic way. A good line-drawn animation can sometimes do a better job of capturing the move-

[7]This paragraph is adapted from "Interface as Mimesis" [Laurel, 1986b].

[8]The Guides project provides a counter-example. The several guides do in fact speak at various points in the program. The desire for I/O symmetry is mitigated by context: The guides are cast as storytellers, embodying a conventional relationship in which one person talks and others listen without interruption. Even so, the product would undoubtedly be improved by the addition of voice input. But if and when it is implemented, then the content and conversational style of that input will need to measure up to those of the computer-enacted agents—a tall order.

ments of a cat than a motion picture, and no photograph will ever capture the essence of light in quite the same way as the paintings of Monet. The point is that first-person sensory and cognitive elements are essential to human-computer activity. There is a huge difference between an elegant, selective multisensory representation and a representation that squashes sensory variety into a dense but monolithic glob of text.

Multisensory experience offers advantages that go beyond engagement, as media theorist Tom Bender describes:

> The kinds of information we receive from our surroundings are quite varied, and have different effects upon us. We obtain raw, direct information in the process of interacting with the situations we encounter. Rarely intensive, direct experience has the advantage of coming through the totality of our internal processes—conscious, unconscious, visceral and mental—and is most completely tested and evaluated by our nature. Processed, digested, abstracted second-hand knowledge is often more generalized and concentrated but usually affects us only intellectually—lacking the balance and completeness of experienced situations. . . . Information communicated as facts loses all its contexts and relationships, while information communicated as art or as experience maintains and nourishes its connections [Bender, 1973].

Bender's observations have been supported quite persuasively by the "multimedia revolution" in computer-based educational activities. Likewise, educational simulations (as opposed to tutorial or drill-and-practice forms) excel in that they present *experience* as opposed to *information*. Learning through direct experience has, in many contexts, been demonstrated to be more effective and enjoyable than learning through "information communicated as facts." Direct, multisensory representations have the capacity to engage people intellectually as well as emotionally, to enhance the contextual aspects of information, and to encourage integrated, holistic responses. This broad view of information subsumes artistic applications, as well as traditional knowledge representation. What Bender calls "direct experience," plus the experience of personal agency, are key elements of human-computer activity.

## Empathy and Catharsis

In drama, we experience empathy with the characters; that is, we experience *vicariously* what the characters in the action seem to be feeling. Empathy is subject to the same emotional safety net as engagement—we experience the characters' emotions as if they were our own, but not quite; the elements of "real" fear and pain are absent. When we are agents in a mimetic action, our emotions about our *own* experiences partake of the same special grace. When I took my five-year-old daughter on the *Star Tours* ride at Disneyland (a wild ride combining flight simulator technology with *Star Wars* content), she turned to me in mid-shriek and shouted, "If this was *real*, I'd be *scared*!"

Even in task-oriented applications, there is more to the experience than getting something done in the real world, and this is the heart of the dramatic theory of human-computer interaction. Our focus is not primarily on how to accomplish real-world objectives but rather how to accomplish them in a way that is both pleasing and amenable to artistic formulation—that is, in a way in which the designer may shape our experience so that it is enjoyable, invigorating, and whole.

When we participate as agents, the shape of the whole action becomes available to us in new ways. We experience it not only as observers or critics but also as comakers and participants. Systems that incorporate this sensibility into their basic structure open up to us a whole new dimension of dramatic pleasure. This is the stuff of dream and desire, of life going *right*. It is the vision that fuels our love affairs with art, computers, and any other means that can enhance and transform our experience.

The experience of pleasure in a whole action is also influenced by how that action is defined or bounded. In the domain of document creation, for instance, my pleasure and satisfaction has been enormously increased by developments in word processing and printing technology that allow me to engage in more of the *whole* action, from inception to final result. In the days of typewriters, one created documents that would be completely transformed in appearance (one hoped) through the process of publication. Through the addition of document design to the application of word processing, and with the assistance of a laser printer, I can now influence the final appearance of a publication through my own (design and formatting) actions, and I can bask in the sense that the thing is really *done* by seeing it in something that closely approximates its published form. We will develop this example further in Chapter 6.

The most complex and rewarding result of dramatic action is *catharsis*, defined by Aristotle as the pleasurable release of emotion. That's not to say that all emotions aroused by a play are necessarily pleasant ones. Pity, fear, and terror are mainstays of noncomic forms. It is not the emotion itself, but its release that is deemed "pleasurable." Furthermore, emotions aroused by a play differ in context and expectation from those experienced in real life. When we are viewing a play or film or even riding a roller coaster, we expect emotions to be aroused and to have the opportunity to release them. Aristotle's point is that emotional arousal and release is intrinsically pleasurable in the special context of representations; indeed, that is one of their primary values to us.

In Chapter 1 we discussed a Brechtian view of catharsis that suggests that emotional closure necessarily takes place beyond the temporal "ending" of a play. Brecht's hypothesis was based on a view that requires the integration of the experience of a play into our ongoing life. Brecht's ideas have been interpreted primarily in a political and social light. Julian Hilton offers a more semiotically inclined view of the same phenomenon:

> The totality of the performed event functions as a means of reflective support to the audience, which by no means stops when the performance itself stops. Indeed, in the case of fundamental mythologic structures, such as the Pygmalion/Galathea mythology to which I referred above, their power derives doubly from their synecdochic property of representing in parable form a common human truth and from their persistence in real time operations of the imagination—that is, the imagination uses such myths in a way similar to programming macros or subroutines. The attraction of reflective support is

> that it accepts and draws interest from the potential for contradictory resolution of any problem and turns the contract of error from a negative one (a loss of truth or of totality in content) into the leading edge of investigation [Hilton, 1991].

Catharsis depends upon the way that probability and causality have been orchestrated in the construction of the whole; it also depends upon our uninterrupted experience of engagement with the representation. More than that, it is the pleasure that results from the completion of a form. The final form of a thing may be suspected from the beginning or unforeseen until the very end; it may undergo many or few transformations. It may be happy or sad, because the "success" of the outcome in terms of the representational content is not nearly so potent as the feeling of completion that is implicit in the final apprehension of the shape of a whole of which one has been a co-creator. The theory of catharsis dictates that no matter how monumental or trivial, concrete or abstract, the representation affords the occasion for the complete expression of those emotions that have been aroused in the course of the action. In plain terms, it means that we must design clear and graceful ways for things to end.

Of all forms of human-computer activity, computer games are both the worst and best at providing catharsis. They are the best when a player or a computer-based opponent wins, and they are the worst when no one wins, but the action is truncated because it could not continue.[9] In task-oriented environments, the trick is to define the "whole" activity as something that can provide satisfaction and closure when it is achieved. This depends in part on being able to determine what a person is trying to do and striving to enable them to do *all* of it. In simulation-based activities, the need for cathar-

---

[9]Here again, it seems that the designers at Lucasfilm are in the forefront. Ron Gilbert counsels game designers to avoid situations in which a player must "die in order to learn what not to do next time." [Gilbert, 1989] In a presentation at SIGGRAPH '90, LucasArts Entertainment's research director Doug Crockford showed a re-edited version of *Star Wars* in which Luke Skywalker was killed in his first battle with Darth Vader. The story was over in less than three minutes.

sis strongly implies that what goes on be structured as a whole action with a dramatic "shape." If I am flying a simulated jet fighter, then either I will land successfully or be blown out of the sky, hopefully after some action of a duration that is sufficient to provide pleasure has had a chance to unfold. Flight simulators shouldn't stop in the middle, even if the training goal is simply to help a pilot learn to accomplish some midflight task. Catharsis can be accomplished, as we have seen, through a proper understanding of the nature of the whole action and the deployment of dramatic probability. If the end of an activity is the result of a causally related and well-crafted series of events, then the experience of catharsis is the natural result of the moment at which probability becomes necessity.

This chapter has analyzed various ways in which dramatic ideas and techniques can be employed to influence the way human-computer activities *feel* to people who take part in them. Hopefully, it has illustrated some of the benefits of a dramatic approach in terms of engagement and emotion. The chapter has emphasized the need to delineate and represent human-computer activities as organic wholes with dramatic structural characteristics. It has also suggested means whereby people experience agency and involvement naturally and effortlessly. The next chapter explores structural techniques more deeply, returning to Aristotle's six elements, and suggesting principles and rules of thumb for designing each of them in the computer domain.

Chapter Five

# *Design Principles for Human-Computer Activity*

## *Designing Action*

Most art forms characteristically involve representations of real-world phenomena. As Aristotle observed, art represents *not what is, but a kind of thing that might be*; environments, objects, situations, characters, and actions are represented within a wide range of deviation from real life. The degree and types of deviations are the result of the form, style, and purpose of the representation. In drama, only a few styles (predominantly of the last two centuries) venture far afield from representing characters, situations, and actions that are recognizably human or human-like. Likewise, nonrepresentational styles in painting and sculpture are largely modern developments that are generally beyond the "mainstream." One reason for the preference for real-world objects in artistic representations, at least in popular culture, may be the fact that they impose relatively less cognitive overhead on their audiences. The principle at work here seems to be that real-world objects make representations more accessible, and hence more enjoyable, to a larger number of people.

Computers have become an interactive, representational medium. Understanding what computers really are is an ongoing definitional process that heavily influences the kinds of representations that we make with them. Their use in such areas as statistical analysis and database management have led to the notion of computers as representers of *information*. Scientists use computers to represent *real-world phenomena* in a variety of ways, from mathematical modeling to simulations that are symbolic, schematic, or realistically multisensory.

The outward and visible signs of computer-based representations—that is, the ways in which they are available to humans—has come to be known as the human-computer interface. The characteristics of the interface for any given representation are influenced by the pragmatics of usage and the principles of human factors and ergonomics, as well as by an overarching definition of what computers are. Interface styles that are indirect—that is, those in which a person's actions are defined as operating the computer rather than operating directly on the objects they represent—spring from the notion that *computers themselves are tools*. The logic behind the "tool metaphor" goes like this: Regardless of what people *think* they are doing (for example, searching a database, playing a game, or designing a cathedral), they are *actually* using their computers as tools to carry out their commands, just like programmers. It follows, then, that what people are seen to be interacting with is the computer itself, with outcomes like database management, document design, learning, or game-playing as secondary consequences of that interaction [Laurel, 1986b].

***Think of the computer, not as a tool, but as a medium.***

This notion of the computer as a tool obviously leads to the construction and inclusion of concepts in all application domains that are inconsistent with the context of the specific representation: file operations, buffers, data structures, lists, and programming-like syntax, for example. For purposes of comparison, think about how people use "real" tools. When you hammer a nail into a board, you do not think about operating the hammer—you think about pounding the nail. But in the computer medium the "tool problem" is compounded by existential recursion: The medium can be used to *represent* tools. Some tools, like virtual paintbrushes, are more or less modeled on real-life objects. Others, like the omnipresent cursor in all of its instantiations, have no clear referents in the real world. It is especially in these cases that interface designers are tempted to represent the tool in terms of computer-based operations that are cognitively and operationally unnecessary to their use. Why? Because the computer-oriented representation is seen as an "honest" explanation of what the tool *is* and how it works, and because that's how the *designer* understands it. We quickly become entangled in a mass of internal mythology in contrast to the notion of "external myth" developed in Rubinstein and Hersh [1984] that we must construct in a largely ad hoc fashion. We fall through the trapdoor into the inner workings of the computer.

***Interface and application should be couched in the same context—namely, the context of the objects, actions, and tools of the representational world.***

## Interface Metaphors: Powers and Limitations

The notion of employing metaphors as a basis for interface design has partially replaced the notion of the computer as a tool with the idea of the computer as a *representer of a virtual world or system,* in which a person may interact more or less directly with the representation. Action occurs in the mimetic context and only secondarily in the context of computer operation. The "desktop metaphor" is the leading example of this interface metaphor, shared by such systems as the Xerox STAR and the Apple Macintosh. Windows, desktops, and the idea of direct manipulation are predominant elements of the metaphor, most of which emerged from work done at Xerox Palo Alto Research Center (PARC). Certainly, the move toward the notion of computers as representers of virtual worlds is a step in the right direction from the perspective of dramatic interaction. Interface metaphors have both strengths and weaknesses, and by examining them we can form a picture of what might be the next step in the evolution of human-computer activity.

The most commonly acknowledged strength of interface metaphors derives from the naturalness and pervasiveness of metaphor in human thought and language [see Lakoff and Johnson, 1980]. Interface researcher Tom Erickson describes how metaphors act as "cognitive hooks" for people:

> A word which is used in a metaphorical way is usually just the tip of the iceberg. A metaphor is an invisible web of terms and associations which underlies the way we speak and think about a concept. It is this extended structure which makes metaphor such a powerful and essential part of our thinking. Metaphors function as natural models, allowing us to take our knowledge of familiar, concrete objects and experiences and use it to give structure to more abstract concepts [Erickson, 1990].

The theory is that, if the interface presents representations of real-world objects, people will naturally know what to do with them.

Folders on a Macintosh desktop are a good example. Folders are containers for documents or files in the real world as well as the virtual one. You open a folder to get something out of it. You can put folders inside of folders inside of folders. You can move folders around on your desk. Some physical properties of "real" folders are absent—they have no weight, they don't make noise when you drop them, and they won't give you paper cuts.[1] But these are "magical" folders that have several additional properties that are not drawn from the real world at all—for example, you can sort their contents by name or date or other criteria, and you can put the same document in two folders at once—well, sort of.[2] But it is precisely with these "magical" differences that problems begin. Ted

---

[1]Even though such properties are not things that anyone would miss, they can sometimes enhance experience. As researcher Steve Gano once said, "deleting a file should be as satisfying as crumpling up a wad of paper" [Gano, personal communication].

[2]There is a problem in versions of the Finder previous to 7.0. If you make changes to one of the copies, the changes will not automatically be made

Nelson's acerbic analysis presents the counterpoint to Erickson's argument:

> Let us consider the "desktop metaphor," that opening screen jumble which is widely thought at the present time to be useful. . . . Why is this curious clutter called a desktop? It doesn't *look* like a desktop; we have to tell the beginner *how* it looks like a desktop, since it doesn't (it might as easily properly be called the Tablecloth or the Graffiti Wall).
>
> The user is shown a gray or colored area with little pictures on it. The pictures represent files, programs, and disk directories which are almost exactly like those for the IBM PC, but now represented as in a rebus. These pictures may be moved around in this area, although if a file or program picture is put on top of a directory picture it may disappear, being thus moved to the directory. Partially covered pictures, when clicked once, become themselves covering, and partially cover what was over them before.
>
> We are told to believe that this is a "metaphor" for a "desktop." But I have never personally seen a desktop where pointing at a lower piece of paper makes it jump to the top, or where placing a sheet of paper on top of a file folder caused the folder to gobble it up; I do not believe such desks exist; and I do not think I would want one if it did [Nelson, 1990].

The problem with interface metaphors, as illustrated by folders and other aspects of the desktop metaphor, is that they are like reality only different. Why should this matter? Because we don't know precisely *how* they are different. If we could really treat interface metaphors like metaphors, they might work. In actuality, interface metaphors are *similes*; whereas a metaphor posits that one thing is another, a simile asserts that one thing is *like* another. But what is being compared to what? Now there is a third part to the representation: the simile (a representational folder), the real-world object (a real folder), and the thing it really *is* (a bundle of functionality

---

to any of the others. System 7.0 attempts to solve this problem by introducing a special kind of "copy" of a file (actually a pointer to the original file), with a slightly different graphical representation. These special copies or "aliases" reflect all changes to a file automatically.

and a data structure). This phenomenon is well illustrated in Nelson's comment above, where he never uses the word folder at all, but refers to it as a "disk directory." The simile becomes a kind of cognitive mediator between a real-world object and something going on inside the computer.

What happens if we try to use interface similes? Alas, we must form mental models of what is going on *inside the computer* that incorporate an understanding of all three parts. The only way to comprehend what the trash can on the Macintosh desktop is doing, for instance, is to form an elaborate mental model of its several disparate functions. In this way, interface metaphors can fail to simplify what is going on; rather, they tend to complicate it.[3] Our "naive physics of computing" comes into play when we must explain to ourselves the ways in which the behavior of mimetic objects differs from the behavior of their real-world counterparts [Owen, 1986].

To put it another way, the problem with interface metaphors (or similes) is that they act as indexes (or pointers) to the wrong thing: the internal operations of the computer. John Seely Brown of Xerox PARC puts it this way:

> It is not enough simply to try to show the user how the system is functioning beneath its opaque surfaces; a useful representation must be cognitively transparent in the sense of facilitating the user's ability to "grow" a productive mental model of relevant aspects of the system. We must be careful to separate physical fidelity from cognitive fidelity, recognizing that an "accurate" rendition of the system's inner workings does not necessarily provide the best resource for constructing a clear mental picture of its central abstractions. [Brown, 1986]

---

[3]Incomplete or incorrect mental models of the inner workings of the machine can also elicit "superstitious" behaviors (of the type that psychologists report in operant conditioning experiments, where pigeons "learn" that they must turn around three times and hop on one foot in order to receive a food pellet, because they happened to do it the first time and it "worked"). For instance, for the first year that I used Multifinder on my Macintosh, I believed that all applications had to be closed before I could shut down, because the first time I shut down without closing all the applications the machine crashed. I thrashed around without a clue as to why the problem occurred and came up with a solution that was based on

I fundamentally agree with Brown's assessment. The term "central abstractions" seems to be roughly equivalent to what I call the representation. The point, then, is that object of the mental model should not be what the computer is doing but what is going on in the representation—the context, objects, agents, and activities of the virtual world.

Another strength of interface metaphors is coherence—all of the elements "go together" in natural ways. Folders go with documents that go with desktops. To the extent that this works, the mimetic context is supported and you can go about your business in a relatively uninterrupted way. But there are two ways to fall off the desktop. One is when you start looking for the other things that "go" with it and you can't find them—filing cabinets, telephones, blotters for doodling and making notes or even an administrative assistant to make some calls or type some letters. The other way to fall off the desktop is to find something on it that doesn't go with everything else, thereby undermining or exploding the mimetic context—for example, a trash can that gobbles up your trash seemingly at random and ejects your disks.[4]

A third, highly rated strength of interface metaphors is their value in helping people learn how to use a system. The difficulty comes in helping a person make a graceful transition from the entry-level, metaphorical stage of understanding into the realm of expert use, where power seems to be concentrated specifically in those aspects of a system's operation where the metaphor breaks down. In this context, the usefulness of a metaphorical approach can be understood as a trade-off between the reduced learning load and the potential cognitive train-wrecks that await down the track.

***Interface metaphors have limited usefulness. What you gain now you may have to pay for later.***

---

some fairly week inferences about what Multifinder was doing. It "worked" so I kept doing it.

[4]I allude, of course, to the famous Macintosh trash can. The NeXT machine's "black hole" icon is an interesting alternative, but *as a metaphor* it suggests a disturbing irreversibility. One can, after all, take things back out of a trash can—usually.

## Alternatives to Metaphor in Design

Nelson offers an attractive alternative to "metaphorics" in what he calls "virtuality." The design of a virtuality is driven not by its likeness to real-world phenomena but purely by *conceptual structure* and *feel*. Nelson's belief is that, if these two elements are clearly understood and well implemented, things with no real-world referents can be successfully represented with computers. He offers this example:

> VisiCalc™, the first spreadsheet program, was a remarkable achievement: not only did it take the business concept of a paper spreadsheet and give it automatic calculation, but its whole structure was a tour de force in the design and balancing of principle. VisiCalc's REPLICATE feature is an excellent example of the abstract nature of the design of principle. To replicate a column *and its formulas* corresponds to nothing that was on earth previously; and by dismissing Metaphoric thinking, it could be designed cleanly with no reference to anything that had come before [Nelson, 1990; for a fuller discussion, see Nelson, 1987, pp. DM 69–71].

Although Nelson would probably disagree out of pure cantankerousness, his notion of virtuality is fundamentally similar to a dramatic notion of representation in at least three ways. First, actions that are quite novel can be effectively represented by establishing causality and probability (the notion of probable impossibility). True, representations may not have any real-world counterparts (as in the example above), but they exhibit clear causal relations—if I do this, that will happen, reliably and consistently. Second, effective representation of such objects or actions requires a sensory (visual or multisensory) component. For instance, Nelson proposes "'wormholes' out of which information can be enticed" as a kind of interconnection among various pieces of information in a hypertext universe. Wormholes constitute "a 'new' principle created to provide a visualization for unseen parts, continuities from the seen to the unseen" [Nelson, 1990]. Third, Nelson's emphasis on "feel" implies that the primary attribute of a representational object is its potential for action of which the human agent is an intrinsic part.

## The Primacy of Action

One shortcoming of many metaphorical interfaces is that their design tends be guided by the goal of representing *objects and relations among them* as opposed to representing *actions*. For example, Microsoft Word 4.0 focuses on representing the hierarchies of operations and environments that are part of its massive universe. It does a much poorer job of representing how its base functionality can be accessed—that is, how to perform *actions*. I have used the "footnote" facility of the product regularly over the last few years. At first I could find no way of reading a footnote that I had previously entered except through hard copy. As demonstrated by the magical "location" in which they are entered, footnotes have a different relationship to the "virtual" document than they do in a printed manuscript—they live "somewhere else." Therefore I reasoned that I could read a previously entered footnote by pretending to be entering another one, in order to enter the magical "footnote space" again. Quite recently I learned that the "Page View" option, located hierarchically appropriately in the "Document" menu, would display the footnote as it would appear on the printed page, merging the footnote space into a larger "printed document space." While teaching this neat trick to a friend who is a novice user of the program, she accidentally double-clicked on the footnote number in the text, and bang!—a trapdoor to the footnote space opened up.[5]

The point of the previous example is that the various actions that my friend and I took to read the footnotes, both the "wrong" and the "right" ones, were in no way suggested by the representation. How might the situation be improved? A potential solution derives from one of Shneiderman's principles of direct manipulation: "continuous representation of objects of interest," or, to put it dramatically, continuous representation of the potential for action. Since "page view" (the

---

[5]This whole line of reasoning assumes that people can't or won't read manuals to learn how to do things—at least not at this level of detail. It's like having to read the English libretto for an Italian opera in a dark theatre, only worse. The context shift is fundamentally intolerable, and any interface designer who thinks it is not has not really investigated how people learn to use programs.

mimetic document) is the representation in which both text and footnote contexts are merged, it could be continuously represented (in miniature form, much like the page in the "borders" representation). Highlighting the section of the document that one is currently working on could be used both to indicate the object of current activities (i.e., the text) and, reversibly, to indicate the desire to act upon a different object (the footnotes).[6]

In her book *Through the Interface: A Human Activity Approach to User Interface Design*, Sussane Bødker asserts that a theory of user interface design must be a subset of a larger theory of human *work* [Bødker, 1990]. The notion of the primacy of work is shared by Donald Norman [1990]. Bødker advocates "transparency," and Norman calls for "direct engagement" with the object of work; that is, the operation of the interface as a cognitively distinct activity goes away. These theories, too, support the notion of the primacy of action in human-computer activity; however, both seem to limit the domain of human-computer activities to those that are identified as work. In Bødker's view, the key to understanding and designing what is going on in a human-computer activity is an understanding of work as human action, from the perspectives of psychology and communication theory.

An extension to these observations is that it is not simply *work* that we do with computers, but *work in a representational context*. And clearly, we do other things with computers, too—we learn, explore, noodle around, play, and entertain ourselves. The theory expressed in this book is not inconsistent with the theories of these cognitive psychologists, but it can coexist harmoniously with them as resources for designers of human-computer activity.

***Focus on designing the action. The design of objects, environments, and characters is all subsidiary to this central goal.***

[6]It is both impractical and unfair to take potshots at isolated features of an integrated interface environment. The purpose of this section is not to "heal" Microsoft Word, but to illustrate a way of thinking about a class of problems.

Action is indeed the primary component of human-computer activity—not environments, interfaces, or objects. But environments, interfaces, and objects are traditionally much easier to conceive of and represent than a quality that is fundamentally invisible, and the structure of which is contested at best. What design techniques can reinforce the primacy of action and provide tools for shaping it?

## Formal and Material Means for Shaping Action

Action can be shaped through both formal and material means. In the previous chapters, we discussed the shape of the action of plays and identified some characteristic types of action in terms of their structural characteristics and their function within the whole. We have seen how the structure of dramatic action affects emotional response and how specific structures can lead to certain kinds of pleasurable experience. Now it is time to think about how we might make use of that structural knowledge.

In my doctoral dissertation, I proposed an architecture for enabling action with a dramatic structure in interactive fantasy environments [Laurel, 1986a]. The task that I set for myself was to determine how to go about building a system that would enable a person to participate in a dramatic action in a relatively unconstrained way, influencing the events and outcomes through his or her choices and actions as a character in the action. Such a system must be responsible for creating, maintaining, and giving sensory representation to environments, objects, and characters. It must be able to understand what the human character is doing and make inferences about the human's goals and plans. It must create incidents in the action, based on what the human and computer-based characters do, in order to create a whole action with a dramatic shape. Basically, the system functions like a playwright working with one bizarre constraint: One of the characters is walking around in the playwright's study, inserting actions and lines of dialogue at will, which must be incorporated into a pleasing dramatic whole.

The architecture that I proposed distributes the intelligence required to perform all these functions to various parts of the system. Computer-based characters, for instance, would require knowledge about their world, the ability to generate and modify goals and plans, and the ability to initiate action. They would also be capable of generating their own physical representations. With some modifications, I believe that the approach I developed in the context of interactive fantasy (IF) could be used to shape dramatic action in other contexts as well.

At the heart of an IF system is an "expert" on dramatic structure and playwriting. This entity, called the Playwright, takes the form of an expert system with knowledge about dramatic form and structure and playwriting heuristics. It also has access to knowledge about the world and the characters in it, including the human character. The task of understanding the system characters is relatively straightforward, since their goals and plans are contained entirely within the system and are the result of computational processes that the Playwright can observe and, to a certain extent, control. However, since the Playwright must use the choices and actions of all the characters, including the human character, as material for plot formulation, it must attempt to represent the human character in roughly the same terms as the system characters. This requires a two-pronged process of ongoing inference about and constraint of the human participant.

The Playwright embodies the force of formal causality in the system. It takes the materials provided by the characters and formulates them into action according to its understanding of the characteristics of "good" dramatic structure. When the human character does something, the system characters who happen to be involved at the moment all generate responses to that action on the basis of their individual traits, goals, and plans. The characters' suggestions for their next actions are submitted to the Playwright for review. The Playwright applies knowledge about the shape of the action so far to generate structural criteria for the "best" next action to the task of evaluating the system characters' suggestions. If there is a good match, the Playwright directs that character to proceed and redirects the other system characters to respond accordingly. If there is no good match, the Playwright can employ story-generation techniques to design and prescribe the next incident to the characters for enactment, or it can tweak the characters' traits or goals or situational variables so as to generate an action that is better suited to the emerging whole (Table 5.1).[7]

The Playwright might employ various kinds of knowledge to determine what is going on. It might apply the kind of informational analysis of the action discussed in Chapter 3 (the modified Freytag analysis). It might, using an understanding of goals and plans, perform a goal-based analysis of the central action and conflicts in order to "parse" the action and create a model of the emerging whole. It might also use less formal playwriting heuristics to nudge the action in the direction of conflict or resolution.

So far, we have talked about the notion of an expert system exerting formal control over the action only in the context of IF—an entertainment form—but it is easy to see how a similar strategy might be used in other contexts as well. Simulations are used for a wide variety of purposes, from training to computer-aided design and engineering. For instance, computer-based simulations are routinely used for training purposes in the nuclear power industry and certain aspects of defense. Learning how to operate a system and make good decisions in crisis situations is a primary use of such systems. Dramatic structure could provide the hooks for introducing elements of complication, crisis, surprise, and reversal, and could also orchestrate human emotional

---

[7] Although my work in interactive fantasy was primarily theoretical, many of the ideas contained in it are actively being pursued in the Oz project at Carnegie Mellon University, under the direction of Professor Joseph Bates. For information about Oz, see Bates [1990].

| | |
|---|---|
| **Model** | Model the plot in progress. Using data from the WORLD MODEL and SYSTEM CHARACTERS, the PLAYWRIGHT analyzes the story and determines the formal characteristics of the plot so far. |
| **Specify** | Specify the formal characteristics of appropriate next incidents. The PLAYWRIGHT formulates specifications for candidate incidents to use as evaluation criteria. |
| **Change** | Change scene, situation, or circumstances if appropriate. |
| **Modify** | Modify the goals, priorities, or information access filters of SYSTEM CHARACTERS if necessary. |
| **Access** | Access proposals for next actions from the SYSTEM CHARACTERS. Proposals include explanations in terms of characters' traits, goals, and planning processes. |
| **Simulate** | Simulate proposed actions and changes to determine their probable effects on the plot. |
| **Evaluate** | Evaluate proposed actions and changes by comparing simulation results to formal specifications. |
| **Mandate** | Mandate next incident when an acceptable candidate cannot be produced through the usual processes. |
| **Formulate** | Formulate script for next incident. |
| **Direct** | Direct the SYSTEM CHARACTERS and the ENACTOR subsystem to enact the script. |
| **Control** | Control its own operation by employing meta-knowledge and self-knowledge to select problem-solving strategies. As a by-product of the CONTROL function, the PLAYWRIGHT can produce explanations and justifications for its decisions. |
| **Remember** | Remember what has happened. A log of the script is created, with associated explanations and justifications. |
| **Learn** | Learn from experience. By noticing how it arrives at good and bad choices, the PLAYWRIGHT can improve its own performance. |

*Table 5.1* **Principal functions of the playwright for an IF system.**

response with greater acuity.[8] Dramatic criteria could provide answers to a variety of questions: What is the optimal moment at which to introduce a system malfunction? What is the most powerful means for leading a person to a particular discovery? How can the effects of the traits of coworkers on the process of crisis management be represented? Training applications that are perhaps less emotionally charged but equally filled with dramatic potential can be found in all aspects of business, including management, production, and even (gasp) sales.

> ***Designing action consists of designing or influencing what kinds of incidents will occur and in what order.***

Simulation is a domain where the idea of composing in the medium of *action* is quite natural and, to a certain extent, already embedded in the way that we conceive of simulation-based activities. Less obvious, perhaps, is the domain of information storage and retrieval. The fact that these are seen as data-intensive applications places the emphasis on information as content. In the worlds of hypertext and hypermedia, a spatial metaphor is the most common means of providing an interface to information: People "navigate" information "spaces" or "worlds." The action, or navigation, is a means to the end of arriving at an informational "place"—a document or node. Beyond internal searching that replicates this process in miniature, there is no clear paradigm in the IR world for what we do once we "get there." The action is obscured by a

[8] An interesting question posed by one of my reviewers is whether a crisis simulation should in fact be "entertaining" to people participating in it. To answer, we must focus not on the powers of entertainment media to provide pleasure but rather on their powers to engage and involve. Notice that the worst accidents in nuclear power plants to date have resulted from bizarre constellations of incidents in which literally everything that could go wrong did go wrong at exactly the wrong time. Modeling such causally related chains of events, complete with their surprises and reversals, is essential in training simulators that are intended to help people learn to deal with such crises. The real question is one of *seriousness,* and how seriously a person takes a simulation depends upon how convincing it is and how it is contextualized in terms of that person's "real" job responsibilities.

spatial metaphor that is primarily an attempt to represent what is going on inside the computer. What if we were to define the action of information retrieval, not as *looking for* something, but *examining* or *experiencing* it? This seemingly innocuous shift in point of view puts the emphasis in an entirely different domain: the action involved in *perceiving, interpreting,* and *experiencing* information. These are activities in which the human agent is typically left alone on the other side of the screen to do . . . well, whatever a person does with information. Presenting information in dramatic form—as an active encounter—provides the means for comprehending and reintegrating these lonely activities into the mimetic context. "Navigation" is an action that is *of the interface,* secondary in terms of the real goal of information retrieval, which is to encounter the information itself. We will explore ways in which dramatic *form* can change the experience of information in the section on multimedia in Chapter 6.

Designers also have material forces at their disposal that can indirectly influence the shape of human-computer action. Multisensory representation is the starting point of material causality. The sensory characteristics of representation both suggest and constrain what is possible in a given mimetic context. This is, in fact, one of the ways in which the "desktop metaphor" is a success; for instance, a visual representation of a folder with certain behavioral traits provides a richer potential for action than a textual hierarchical directory. Through its direct-manipulation characteristics, the desktop enriches the experience of agency by adding kinesthetic components.

Most contemporary interfaces present an extremely impoverished "language" for human-computer communication. Linguistic expression is severely constrained by menus, "legal" manipulations, or even natural-language parsers—at least those with small vocabularies and inelegant methods for handling failures.[9] Whether or not we believe in the possibili-

---

[9]Yes, robust natural-language processing is hard—but plenty of existing work demonstrates that it's *possible,* and nothing speeds up a research effort like a lot of good applications waiting to use it (and the research dollars that the potential sellers of those applications can be persuaded to ante up).

ty of robust natural-language processing, there are huge advances that can be made in "natural" language interaction that require only our willingness to apply existing theory and technology. The work of Buxton, Brennan, Schmandt, and Hovy will be reviewed in the section on language and communication later in this chapter. Suffice it to say that the richer the forms of communication available, the richer the potential for the formulation of thought, character, and action.

# *Designing Character and Thought*

## The Man Behind the Curtain

Who or what is the source of these messages?

```
Please insert the disk, "Chapter 2."
Are you sure?
Attempting contact with network.
MacDraw II has unexpectedly quit.
I DON'T KNOW THAT WORD.
```

Who or what is the receiver of these messages?

```
Clean up selection.
Format disk.
Check spelling.
Quit.
```

Who is the agent of these actions?

```
Logon.
Save.
Format paragraph.
Delete *.*.
```

And now, for the $64,000 question: Who said the following?

```
Pay no attention to the man behind the curtain.
```

Without clear agency, the source and receiver of messages in a system are vague and may cause both frustration and serious errors. Without clear agency, the meaning of information may be seriously misconstrued. Without clear agency, things that happen are often as "magical" and fraudulent as the light show created by the Wizard of Oz—and the result of accidental unmasking can be unsettling and may change (as it did for Dorothy and her friends) the whole structure of probability and causality in action.

### *Represent sources of agency.*

There are two primary problems involved in the characteristically vague way that agency is often handled in human-computer activity today. The first is that unclear or "free-floating" agency leaves uncomfortable holes in the mimetic context—holes that people can fall through to find themselves in the twilight zone of system operations where there is no "interface" at all. The second is that these vague forces destroy the *experience* of agency for humans. Typically, these sorts of transactions require that people set parameters or specify the details of a desired action in some way, but the *form* of the transaction is one of supplication rather than cooperation—you might as well apply to Central Services for permission to sit down. As the Cowardly Lion says, "let me at 'im"—let me confront the source of all this bossing around, face to face. Unclear agency places the locus of control in a place where we can't "get at it." Even though we are in fact *agents* by virtue of making choices and specifying action characteristics, these shadowy forces manage to make us feel that we are *patients*—those who are done unto rather than those who do.

The alternative, of course, is to represent agency in the form of character. As we defined it in Chapter 2, character consists in coherent bundles of traits that predispose agents to act in certain ways. That chapter provides definitional information for agents, and the following section offers some guidelines for design.

## Anthropomorphism

In earlier writings, I have listed and attempted to answer many objections to anthropomorphism in computer-based agents [Laurel, 1989; Laurel et al., 1990; Laurel, 1990]. A useful point that has perhaps not been made in the course of the ongoing controversy is the distinction between the personification of the *computer* and the representation of anthropomorphic agents within larger representational contexts supported by the computer medium. Suchman [1987] observes that "the personification of the machine is reinforced by the ways in which its inner workings are a mystery, and its behavior at times surprises us." Whatever its cause, many designers and thinkers find the phenomenon to be undesirable. Turkle [1984] believes that it is important to both the self-esteem and the social behaviors of children to avoid personification of the machine. Shneiderman [1988] adds that personifying the computer is a deception that will eventually be discovered, causing a person to feel badly treated. He goes on to allow that "For young children a fantasy character such as a teddy bear or a busy beaver can be a useful guide through the material. A cartoon character can be drawn and possibly animated on the screen to add visual appeal."

Throughout this book, I have argued, not for the personification of the computer, but for its invisibility. We have treated computers, not as "intelligent" objects, but as a medium through which representational worlds may be experienced. The representation of agents or characters is a different idea altogether than the notion of "personified" computers. There is no evidence to suggest that computer-based characters, no matter what the degree of lifelikeness, lead people to believe that either the machine or the characters themselves are actually alive. In cartoons, movies, and human-computer activities (such as Bright Star's *Talking Tiles* program, which features a digitized, lip-synched video image of a human), children may assume that the characters are "alive"—that is, that they exist outside of the representational context. But they do not typically perceive the representations *themselves* as being alive. When my daughter was four years old, playing with *Talking Tiles*, she remarked about the agent, "I'd like to meet that guy. I'd like to hear him say some other things."

After early childhood, context and media conventions assist adults in distinguishing between representations of characters and representations of "real people" (as in the evening news). It can be argued that the "docudrama" style that has arisen in television is a pernicious development because it obscures that distinction. One important justification of a dramatic approach to the design of agents, as opposed to an attempt to model human personalities, is that we can exploit the powers of both human portrayal and dramatic representation (recall Hilton's Galathea analogy from Chapter 1). Finally, anthropomorphic representation is not a requirement of character or agency, although it may be the appropriate choice for a given realm of action or functionality.

## Designing Agents[10]

The most direct material way to influence action is through the shaping of character and thought. On the system side, this consists of designing and rendering traits, both external and internal, for the various sources of agency. External traits function as "shorthand" for implying internal traits, and they are often based on the artful orchestration of stereotypes [Schank and Lebowitz, 1979; Carbonell, 1980]. Internal traits are the thought processes and predispositions to act that underlie an agent's choices and actions. Internal traits may or may not "match" in any literal way the computational basis of an agent's behavior; they are those traits that the designer wishes people to *infer* from the external traits and behaviors of constructed agents. Remember, the representation is all there is. The case for modeling system-based agents after dramatic characters is based on both the familiarity of dramatic characters as a way of structuring thought and behavior and the

---

[10] Portions of this section are adapted with permission from Laurel [1990].

body of theory and methodology already in place for creating them.

*Think of agents as characters, not people.*

Somewhat ironically, dramatic characters are better suited to the roles of agents than full-blown simulated personalities. Most cultures have a notion of dramatic form, and people are quite familiar with both the differences and similarities between characters and real people. The art of creating dramatic characters is the art of selecting and representing only those traits that are appropriate to a particular set of actions and situations [Schwamberger, 1980]. For many uses, a system-based agent must pass a kind of anti-Turing test in order to be effective. People want to know that the choices and actions of agents who function *on their behalf* in the performance of some role or task will not be clouded by complex and contradictory psychological variables. People often want to be able to *predict* the actions of such agents with greater certainty than those of real people. All agents must be represented in such a way that the appropriate traits are apparent and the associated styles and behaviors can be successfully employed to establish probability and causality. Too much "noise" in the system (that is, too much complexity in character—as would probably result from an "accurate" model of human personality) makes probability and causality harder to deploy in the formulation of action.

Although designers and scholars like Alan Kay worry that oversimplification of character will destroy the illusion of lifelikeness [Kay, 1984], the fact is that, thanks to well-internalized dramatic convention, we can enjoy (and believe in) even one-dimensional dramatic characters. In fact, when a minor dramatic character possesses only one or two actionable traits, audience members will impute elaborate histories and motivations as needed to make it believable [Schwamberger, 1980]. Whether the character is as simple as the Roadrunner or as complex as Hamlet, we take pleasure when—and *only* when—even the surprises in a character's behavior are causally related to its traits.

The selectivity and causality inherent in the structure of dramatic characters simplifies the task of representing agents computationally [Laurel, 1986b]. In the area of story generation, James Meehan, Michael Lebowitz, and others have created functional and entertaining characters from a small cluster of well-conceived traits that are realized as goal-formulating and problem-solving styles [Meehan, 1976; Lebowitz, 1984; Turner, 1990]. Increasingly in the world of adventure and role-playing computer games, designers are implementing characters with traits that are *dynamic* (modified by learning and experience) and *relational* (modified in relation to objects and situations). Notable examples are provided by *Hidden Agenda* by TRANSFiction Systems (see Color Plate IV), and *Maniac Mansion* and *Zak McKracken and the Alien Mindbenders* by Lucasfilm Games. These types of traits suggest the ability of agents to learn—itself a kind of trait.

A character is coherent—whole—when its traits are well-integrated through careful selection and planned interaction. Designers can look to the considerable body of work on playwriting for guidance, as well as to the areas of story generation and computer games.

Well-designed system-based agents can contribute to dramatic engagement, elicit empathy, and influence the actions and emotional responses of human agents involved in the same activity. The Guides project of the Advanced Technology Group at Apple (described briefly in Chapter 1) provides a good example. From its inception, the project aimed at investigating the value of anthropomorphic agents in suggesting next moves in a database on the basis of their "interests." In the earliest version, these agents were represented as graphical icons and their suggestions were derived from "hard" links in the HyperCard database. A second version added an emphasis on point of view as an epistemological issue and attempted to establish a narrative rather than a spatial metaphor for information retrieval in the hypernet. In an attempt to pursue these goals, a video dimension was added to the representation of one of the guides. For several topics in the database, the guide had stories to tell (in video format) that were based on her character's experiences and point of view.

With the second version, it was discovered almost by accident that the guide was also evoking feelings of companionship and support in many people who used the prototype:

> In the video version, users were introduced to the Settler guide in a segment where the actress appeared out of costume. Because she was charged with delivering information about the operation of the system and the interface at this juncture, the guide spoke "out of character." We discovered through user testing that users did not even identify the guide in this segment as the same *actress*, and that they imbued her with an entirely different set of traits and functions. They expected this guide to provide help throughout their use of the program, and they perceived the guide as being an ever-present "safety net" and companion [see Karimi et al., 1989]. *All of these user responses were based on a single non-interactive video segment of less than two minutes in length.* What began for the designers as a framing device aimed at distinguishing levels of activity quickly became the beginnings of a distinct type of agent: a *frame guide* [Laurel et al., 1990].

The third version of Guides pursued these findings and also made several enhancements to the "intelligence" of the agents, described in the section on multimedia design in Chapter 6.

The character and thought of *human* agents may be designed to a certain extent as well, and constitutes an integral part of the materials of the whole action. Systems must capture and respond to key traits of human agents. They may also transform human traits or even endow a person with new traits in order to enhance his or her ability to act in the mimetic world. For instance, a system might not be able to "perceive" your physical traits, but it could enable you to *create* the "physical" representation of yourself that would be seen by other people in the mimetic universe. This technique precisely has been used in *Habitat*, a network environment that was introduced in Japan on Fujitsu's FM Towns machines in 1990, designed by Chip Morningstar, Randy Farmer, Aric Wilmunder, and Gary Winnick at Lucasfilm Games in 1986-88. (*Habitat* was originally developed to run on Commodore-64 computers via the Quantum Link network.)

In *Habitat*, the person and the system collaborate on constructing a "physical" (multisensory) representation for the person (Color Plate V). It is this representation that other people see during network interaction. Logically, people can present different physical traits to different individuals with whom they come in contact on the network. People can change gender and age as well as general attractiveness in their (sometimes multiple) self-representations.

*Habitat* illustrates another approach to agent design: the notion of allowing people to design their *own* agents. An agent that is responsive to the goals, needs, or preferences of a person—and especially an agent that can "learn" to adapt its behaviors and traits to the person and the unfolding action—could be said to be "codesigned" by the person and the system. The agent Eager, discussed in Chapter 4, is a strong example of such codesign. The NewWave operating system released for Hewlett-Packard computers in 1990 features a user-programmable agent:

> The NewWave Agent (represented by the icon of a man with shades) is like a servant who acts for the user. The user writes a Task Language script that is handed to the Agent for execution. These scripts are special objects called Agent Tasks. [Chew, 1990]

It is laudable that HP users can get the NewWave Agent to do things for them, but having to do so by writing programs seems, in some ways, to defeat the purpose. For many people (and I'm one of them), writing the program is more difficult, distracting, and tedious than doing the task that I would have delegated to the agent.

***An agent should be both responsive and accessible.***

In the Guides project, we learned that people often wanted to create agents "from scratch." Teachers wanted to create guides that would nudge students in the direction of curricular goals, and kids were interested in creating guides to represent themselves to others—to insert their own points of view into the representational world. We developed the notion of "custom guides" and implemented a means whereby people could create them. The basic predispositions to act—that is, to make suggestions about information to look at in the database based on both the guide's point of view and the person's current interest—were embedded in *the notion of* custom guides. People could name a guide, then ask it to be interested in several topics and perhaps selected media types (Color Plate VI). The custom guide would then be available to make suggestions on the display screen. As an additional means of "training" the guide, we decided to enable people to tell a custom guide to remember any item that appeared in the display window. Future enhancements might include a means for creating or importing graphical representations for custom guides and adding point-of-view stories for the custom guides to the database. (The ability to add *anything* to a multimedia database, if it is stored on optical media, is a key obstacle to be overcome in the design of future multimedia hardware and software.)

# Designing Language and Communication

In Aristotelian terms, language serves as the material for thought, which is in turn formulated into character. In the previous section we described how thought and character can be designed in relation to their formal cause: The action that is being represented. Now we turn to their material cause—language—in which concepts are embedded and through which we come to know the higher-level structures of meaning that they represent.

## Language Generation

In cases in which agents use language, the problem of I/O symmetry must be addressed. The Guides example in Chapter 4 illustrates the use of context to mitigate the desire to "talk back" to characters that can speak. Language generation may be desirable in order to create diction for characters and also to create descriptive or narrative "glue" that holds a story-like action together.

The Oz project at Carnegie Mellon [see Bates, 1990] provides examples of both of these uses. Oz currently employs a text-only interface to create interactive stories. The decision to employ a text interface was a logistical one, allowing the designers to concentrate on the AI-based problems of generating stories. It is the hope of the Oz researchers that at a later point in the system's development, a virtual-reality style interface can be employed. But as the medium of interactive representations evolves, it may be that text and pictures will coexist in new ways in new interactive forms. The examples of *Habitat* (in this chapter) and *Monkey Island* (in Chapter 4) show how text and pictures can be comfortably integrated into a single representational context. Furthermore, natural-language–like descriptions of the type that are being used in the Oz project could be used to drive the construction and orchestration of animations within the system. Oz researcher Mark Kantrowitz [1990] has developed a natural-language text generation system that can theoretically serve both purposes.

When character dialogue is employed, it is, of course, important to vary characters' diction in order to represent traits, predispositions, and point of view. One of the future goals of the Guides project is to reformulate the diction employed in text articles to reflect different points of view. The production and presentation of alternative representations of information is a key capability for computer-based agents in the future, especially in information-retrieval–based applications. The work of Eduard Hovy of the Information Sciences Institute of the University of Southern California shows extraordinary promise in creating character-specific diction from a single, "base" form of a piece of information. Hovy's system, called PAULINE, is capable of creating distinctly different descriptions of the same events with the same "factual content" that vary according to speaker characteristics, hearer characteristics, mutual relationships, mutually understood concepts, medium of communication, and physical and social context. PAULINE represents these differences as fourteen "rhetorical goals," including such characteristics as formality, partiality, force, haste, detail, and verbosity [Hovy, 1988 and 1990]. The results are widely differing linguistic representations that reveal character and point of view.

***Match diction to character traits. Diction can also be used to reveal point of view.***

An important point to remember is to avoid the representation of traits through diction that do not exist in terms of an agent's behavior. False politeness is a common flaw in many interfaces, and one that I find especially irritating. Linguist Susan Brennan [1990a] cites the example of an on-line library catalog where the system uses the word "please." The person dutifully responds in the same polite fashion and the system informs her that "please" is not a word it recognizes, creating problems on the levels of language, thought, and character. Another example is an automated bank teller machine that asks a person politely to "please wait" [Rubinstein and Hersh, 1984]. Of course, the person has no other choices (except to walk away from the machine in midtransaction). Here, the language glitch is most apparent at the level of action.

## Conversationality

As Brennan observes, "people's expectations about human/computer interaction are often inherited from what they expect from human/*human* interaction" [Brennan, 1990a]. Suchman provides a concurring perspective:

> Insofar as the machine is somewhat predictable . . . and yet is also both internally opaque and liable to unanticipated behavior, we are more likely to view ourselves as engaged in interaction with it than as just performing operations upon it, or using it as a tool to perform operations upon the world (see MacKay 1962) [Suchman, 1987].

Rubinstein and Hersh [1984] provide further corroboration in the form of a report of an executive's transaction with the famed ELIZA program. The executive was convinced that he was conversing with a programmer at a remote terminal. Rubinstein and Hersh observe that people who are not similarly predisposed to think that they are talking to a human exhibit the same tendency to treat human-computer interaction as human-human interaction: "Their candor suggests a sincerity of interaction that is usually reserved for other people, not computer programs. People are having *conversations* with the computer."

Brennan's thesis is that a model of human conversation can be used to understand why some interface features work and some do not, as well as to provide principles that can be used in the design of human-computer activity. She asserts that "the fundamental ability of human beings to adapt to their conversational partners makes the whole human/computer enterprise possible." She provides experimental evidence to support the thesis that "the way a conversational partner represents itself and the style in which it responds influences how a person designs utterances for that partner," no matter whether that partner is human or computer-based. She presents the following strategies for designing human-computer communication based on the characteristics of human-human conversation:

> (1) Don't continue until an understanding that is sufficient for current purposes is reached. (2) Assume that errors will happen and provide ways to negotiate them. (3) Articulate the answer or response in a way that preserves the adjacency with (and apparent relevance to) the question or command. (4) Represent the interface in a way that invisibly constrains the user to act in ways the system understands and to stick to the application domain. (5) Integrate typed input with pointing and other input/output channels. Applying these strategies should make interaction with a computer more *conversational*, whether it's via a desktop or a natural language interface [Brennan, 1990a].

Although Brennan does not distinguish any agency beyond the general agency of the computer in this study, her observations can be effectively applied in the construction of conversational behavior for agents who possess widely diverse traits. The only exceptions would seem to be agents whose characters are (for some solid mimetic reason) poor communicators, or antipathetic to human agents in some way. Brennan's point (4) above speaks to the issue of intrinsic constraints, and her research shows that people tend to emulate the conversational styles of their partners, to the end of improving conversational effectiveness. Presumably, because conversation involves negotiated meaning and common ground (as discussed in Chapter 1), conversational partners also constrain each other to "stick to the subject."

***Modeling human conversational style is important, but remember that people readily adapt to and emulate the conversational styles of their partners.***

Brennan's point (5) recommends the coupling of speech with gesture (in particular, pointing) to achieve conversationality. The realm of gestural communication will be discussed in the next section. In the multileveled mimetic context of human-computer activity, we might logically extend Brennan's observation to include more than those actions of agents that are directly related to interagent communication. For instance, actors who are involved in improvisation accommodate one another in strikingly similar ways, not only in the realm of direct communication but in all aspects of agency—for example, nongestural movement, thought, and implicit collaboration on the shape of the evolving plot. This is part of the "cognitive overhead" of theatrical improvisation that I intended to address with the IF architecture I proposed in my dissertation. An interactive fantasy system (and, by extension, any interactive representation) must possess the means to eliminate any need for conscious collaboration on the part of human agents in the *formal* shaping of plot. Such formal concerns interfere with direct engagement and are out of place in any human-computer activity. That is the reason for stressing the system's role as the locus of top-down formal causality in shaping the action, as discussed in the first section of this chapter.

In drama, both playwrights and actors employ such principles of conversationality as those articulated by Brennan. Playwrights employ them in the construction of dialogue utterances. Actors employ them in the representation of back-channels—feedback that an utterance has or has not been understood—in the form of gestures, postural changes, facial expressions, and such nonverbal utterances as "um-hmm." Thus the conversational model can be seen to apply to mimetic as well as "natural" contexts.

Interesting examples of the application of some of the principles that Brennan discusses can be found in two of the systems created by Chris Schmandt and others at the MIT Media Laboratory. The *Phone Slave* telephone messaging system (discussed in Chapter 5) employs the notion of *adjacency pairs* in terms of questions and answers to implicitly constrain humans in the content and style of information that they provide [Schmandt and Arons, 1985]. As Schmandt observes, this system is built on the simple premise that when you ask people questions, they tend to give you answers; that is, the system is probably safe in making the assumption that the utterance following a question is an answer. The *Grunt* system, which assists people in reaching destinations by driving a car, manages to evoke and shape conversational responses from people principally through the understanding of paralinguistic features like utterance length and the duration of pauses, as well as through the use of "back-channel" utterances like "huh?" ("grunts"). This remarkably simple, nonlexical representation is so successful in capturing the essence of conversation that people often imbue the "system" (or grunt agent) with much higher "intelligence," especially in terms of its ability to understand natural language, than it actually possesses [Schmandt, 1987].

## "Natural" Language

Schmandt's work raises the issue of the essential characteristics of natural language. Must it involve words? Must it be spoken at all? Must it involve things besides words? Designer and researcher William Buxton presents an alternate view of what constitutes natural language:

> We argue that there is a rich and potent gestural language which is at least as "natural" as verbal language, and which—in the short and long term—may have a more important impact on facilitating human-computer interaction. And, despite its neglect, we argue that this type of language can be supported by existing technology, and so we can reap the potential benefits immediately [Buxton, 1990].

Gestural languages take many forms and present both benefits and challenges in the context of human-computer activity. Beyond such highly conventionalized gestural systems as American Sign Language or the gestural lexicons of football referees or conductors, "routine" human gestures are "fuzzier" than writing or speech. While some gestures are highly conventionalized and explicitly semiotic (such as waving goodbye), others are highly idiosyncratic and expressive. In the domain of acting, where it would be especially useful to know a "vocabulary" of gestures that would be guaranteed to communicate the proper information or emotion, only one serious attempt has been made to create a "universal" gestural language—the work of Delsarte in the nineteenth century [Stebbins, 1886]. When we look at Delsarte's gestural language today, we are immediately struck by its artificial conventionality, and some of it seems to make no sense at all (for instance, Delsarte's gesture for surprise is both arms extended vertically in the air).

The creation of gesture to convey both information and emotion is a central feature of the actor's art. Although conventions governing gestural clarity and visibility can be learned by rote, the art of finding and executing an effective gesture is learned through the more indirect means of observation, experimentation, performance, and evaluation, and it is a skill that continues to grow over time.

***Gesture can be used to reinforce, disambiguate, or replace spoken or written language.***

Although a universal gestural language has not been identified, gestural input that is not strictly semiotic in its intent can be interpreted by computer systems. Margaret Minsky of the MIT Media Laboratory has created a system that employs gestural input to manipulate objects in a graphical display. Minsky's system utilizes a touch-sensitive display and employs a notion of "gesture parsing" that could be utilized in three-dimensional representations.[11] Her system uses two-dimensional gestural data to classify gestures according to their intent (selecting something, moving something, or indicating a path). The gesture is interpreted through the use of information about its trajectory, the nearest object, the pressure applied to the display, changes in pressure over time, and other factors [Minsky, 1984]. Minsky has expanded her research on gesture to include how things push back, technically described as force feedback [Minsky, 1990].

Buxton suggests one solution to the problems posed by the search for a universal gestural language through the use of context-specific gestural sets:

> So-called natural languages are only natural to those who have learned them. All others are foreign. If we start to consider non-verbal forms of communication, the same thing holds true. The graphic artist's language of using an airbrush, for example, is foreign to the house painter. Similarly, the architectural drafts person has a language which includes the use of a drafting machine in combination with a pencil. Each of these "languages" is natural (albeit learned) for the profession [Buxton, 1990].

The nature of the task and the form of the representation presented to people can serve to constrain the intentionality

---

[11] "Parsing" is a term that usually refers to the process of breaking a sentence into its component parts of speech and describing their grammatical and syntactic relations. The notion of "gesture parsing" suggests that gestures may be interpreted in much the same way as words or sentences. It implies that specific, recognizable gestures have specific meanings, that the parts of gestural expressions and their syntactic relations can be identified. The existence of such semantic and syntactic elements is persuasively demonstrated in various systems of sign language.

and physical characteristics of the gestures that they are likely to employ. In a given situation, a person employs a limited set of gestures, some of which are stereotypical (e.g., "dukes up" in a fistfight). A human-computer system might call upon various limited gestural vocabularies at various points in the action, much as a speech recognizer might employ contextual cues to select and load a limited recognition vocabulary.[12] Thus one gestural "vocabulary" might be used in the context of informal conversation, while others could be provided for situations in which movement is more formalized, such as a courtroom scene or a duel.

Such gestural languages are available for many contexts that are likely to be the subject of computer-based mimesis, such as editing, drawing, painting, animating, and conducting or performing music. Furthermore, it is likely that the human use of gestures in human-computer activity can be constrained in the same way as utterance style is constrained among conversational partners; that is, partners tend to emulate one another's styles. The representation of gestures by system-based agents can be constrained through the use of gestural qualities that derive from character traits and emotional states; for instance, the speed, force, and abruptness or percussiveness of gestures can be orchestrated to suggest such qualities as anger, assertiveness, gentleness, or lethargy. When overlaid on a relatively small set of stock gestures that are unique to individual agents, these parameters can create effective distinctions among them. In the most recent version of the Guides project, for instance, each of the four guides has four "stock" gestures and postures to indicate degrees of interest in the item of information that is currently being displayed. Each of the four gestures is individually tailored to suggest other character traits. The result is a lively screen

[12] Psychologist and philosopher Manfred Clynes has developed a system called *sentics,* which purports to measure the "characteristic waveforms" of emotions. Clynes contends that a distinctive shape is somehow genetically associated with each of the basic human emotions, and purports to have found evidence for his theory in laboratory experiments, as well as in music, painting, dance, and other art forms [Clynes, 1977].

filled with a seemingly wide variety of activity that is enhanced by personalization and juxtaposition (Color Plate VII).

Gesture can be used as a principal—or even the only—component of language in a human-computer activity. The technical and creative challenges inherent in gesture are relatively less complex than those inherent in complete natural-language processing. Gestures are especially useful in establishing orientation, pointing, making connections, and grouping objects [Kurtenbach and Hulteen, 1990]. They can also enhance the experience of agency through kinesthetic involvement and the feeling of directness. Gestures are effective as a secondary channel in disambiguating speech [Schmandt and Hulteen, 1982]. As with other aspects of human-computer activity, dramatic selectivity can be used to simplify the design of gestures without detracting from mimetic experience.

Body language such as posture and positional changes can be employed to augment or amplify explicit communication, as well as to suggest character traits [see, for instance, Fast, 1971, for a description and analysis of body language]. Human body language can be captured by the same sort of tracking devices that are employed in tracking gestures; for instance, input from the VPL DataSuit—a piece of clothing that senses the positions of head, torso, and limbs—could be used with pattern-matching software to make gross discriminations among postures and to drive inferences about their significance in relation to context. Also, the "pointing" function of gaze—that is, where a person is looking—can be captured by eye-tracking technology. Body language and pointing-by-looking can be represented as part of the behavior of computer-based characters as well.

Communication in human-computer activities is constrained not only by the computing power devoted to the problem and the software techniques employed but also by the bandwidth and media of the representation. We have said that, by its very nature, human-computer activity should involve multisensory representation. That is not to say, however, that all human-computer activities should involve all modalities all the time, or that they need to represent a particular modality in a "realistic" way. The selection and treatment of various modalities is the subject of the next section.

# *Designing Enactment*

How does a designer determine what sensory modalities to incorporate in a human-computer activity? Beyond the constraints imposed by hardware, are there selection criteria that can be of use? Are there any guiding principles regarding the integration of multiple modalities in representations?

## Selecting and Integrating Multiple Modalities

The primary criterion for deciding which sensory modalities should be part of a representation is *appropriateness to the action,* in both mimetic and operational terms. Does a drawing activity need to involve the kinesthetic sense? Almost certainly, since drawing is itself a kinesthetic as well as a visual activity. Does a drawing program need to support speech input? A colleague who often argues against speech interfaces once quipped, "if MacDraw had a speech interface, people would use it to say things like 'move the little hand up' (a reference to the absurd notion of using speech to control a tool for pointing and manipulation). But what if the activity involves the frequent changing of drawing tools? Contemporary "direct manipulation" interfaces to drawing programs confine the activity to a visual and kinesthetic universe, constraining a person to point at a menu or execute a keyboard command. It might be more appropriate for the representation to allow a person to specify a new tool by speaking its name, thereby preserving continuity and direct engagement in the activity of drawing. How about musical accompaniment? If one of the motivations of a person involved in the activity is to create animations with a musical score, then music is a necessary element of the representation.

***Multiple modalities are desirable only insofar as they are appropriate to the action being represented.***

The latter example illustrates the function of enactment in providing materials that are used in the formulation of the action. These materials delimit the potential for action in a mimetic world. Through the workings of material causality, they also constrain the traits of both human and computer-based agents in the action. If an agent cannot employ language (either through text, speech, or gesture), for instance, then certain concepts cannot be expressed and certain actions cannot be represented. For example, the aspect of three-dimensionality in visual representations creates the potential for a wider range of "physical" action in the environment; that is, things can move forward and backward as well as right and left, and "moving around" in a variety of new ways becomes possible for the agents.

In the use of multiple sensory modalities, causal relations must be taken into account. Let's use sound as an example. If "natural" sound (as opposed to speech or music) is an aspect of an environment, it must be employed consistently; that is, the causal relationships between sound and other modalities must be preserved. When things fall down (in a world that has sounds), they go "boom." Causality also applies to the relations among qualitative elements—for example, the relationship between sound and character as part of enactment. My Mac II clears its throat at me when I ask it to do something it can't understand. I endowed my operating system with this trait because I hated the officious little "ding" that it provides by default. I prefer the anthropomorphic "ahem" —its polite deference to my concentration, its seeming hesitance to interrupt. It is also quite clearly a *male* "ahem," which I find consistent with other aspects of the behavior of the OS. In this example, the sound provides material for the character I am constructing, and the traits of that character exert a formal influence on the sound. This little wisp of character and its simple action influence how I perceive and feel about all of the actions that I informally attribute to the same "agent," my

Mac II system software, which hangs around in the background even when some other agent (like that knuckle-cracking Nun that presides over my Unix-based electronic mail system) has center stage.

Preserving causal relations (and making the most of them) promotes integration and synergy among modalities. For instance, close coupling of the visual and kinesthetic senses permits very convincing and engaging representations of motion through such techniques as motion parallax. In head-mounted virtual-reality displays, the key to the person's sense of being "in" or "surrounded by" the representation environment is primarily the result of visual-kinesthetic coupling; when I turn my head, the room "moves" accordingly; when I move forward, the world flows by in visually realistic ways.

***Tight linkage between visual, kinesthetic, and auditory modalities is the key to the sense of immersion that is created by many computer games, simulations, and virtual-reality systems.***

In a somewhat less sophisticated representational world, William Gaver's *Sonic Finder*, a prototype version of the Macintosh Finder that incorporates sound, the sounds that objects make when they are manipulated reinforce and amplify the simplistic three-dimensionality suggested in the visual representation and also provide additional feedback for a person's kinesthetic activities [Gaver, 1989]. Gaver has employed a similar technique in creating an auditory component for SoundSHARK, a virtual physics lab developed by Randy Smith of Xerox EuroPARC [Gaver and Smith, 1990] (Figure 5.1).

In integrating media in a representation, it is often necessary to transfer some of the qualities of one medium to another with which it is being integrated, or to create a representational context in which they can comfortably coexist. The former technique is perhaps best illustrated in the way that video and animation are integrated in the 1989 Disney film *Who Framed Roger Rabbit?* This was not the first film to

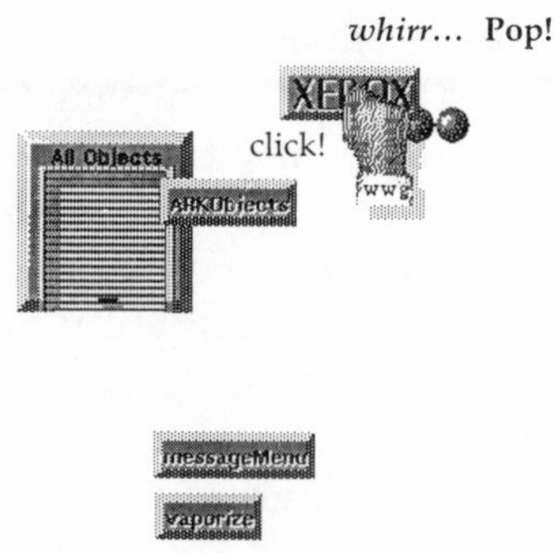
whirr... Pop!
click!
All Objects
ARKObjects
wwg
messageMenu
vaporize

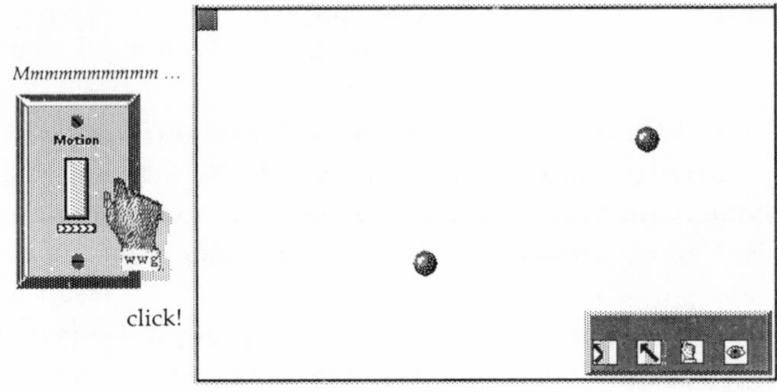
Mmmmmmmmmm ...
Motion
wwg
click!

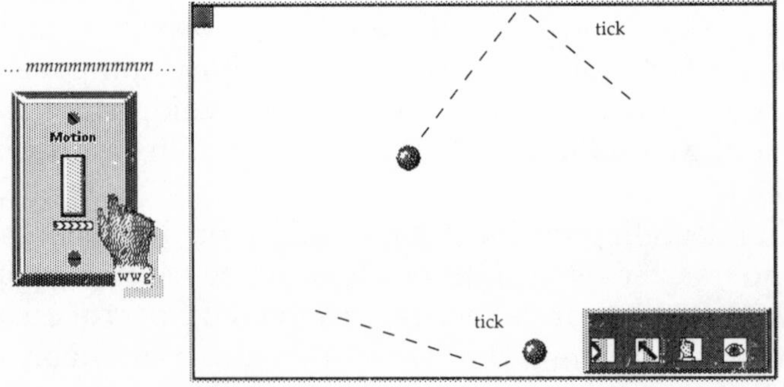
... mmmmmmmmm ...
Motion
wwg
tick
tick

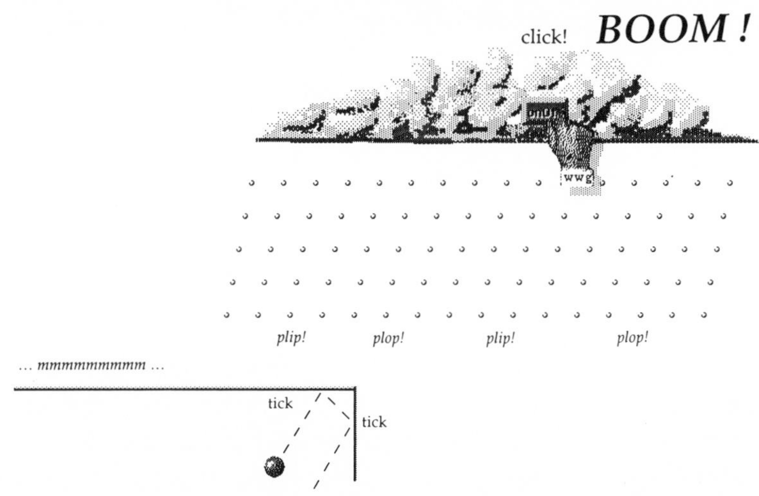


*Figure 5.1* **An annotated representation of the use of sounds in SoundSHARK, produced by William Gaver and Randy Smith at Xerox EuroPARC.** SoundSHARK combines graphics and sound in a simulated physics laboratory. For instance, in (a), a person copies a ball with a Xerox button; the button makes a machinelike sound as the ball pops into existence. In (b), the user has placed the balls inside a room. When she turns on the law of motion, a click confirms her act and a constant hum indicates that motion is "on." As the balls bounce around the room (c), they make sounds as they hit the walls. These sounds can be heard even when the user moves to a different part of the system (d). When she activates a raincloud (click!), thunder booms, and raindrops splash.

attempt such integration; it was used in Disney's *Song of the South* nearly fifty years earlier. But the action in *Song of the South* (as well as the scenes that combine the two media similarly in *Mary Poppins* and other films) jumps back and forth from a filmic "realistic" context to an animated "make-believe" one, depending upon which element predominates in a given scene. *Roger Rabbit* succeeds in suggesting that the two types of representations belong to the same world, regardless of which happens to be the dominant element at any given moment. This is accomplished by endowing all of the animated representations with enhanced three-dimensionality (especially in terms of light modeling and motion characteristics) and by extending the effects of movement and gesture across media (people shoot cartoon guns, animated characters break filmic windows).

Ralph Bakshi's film treatment of *The Lord of the Rings* illustrates another approach to combining modalities by blending film and animation through the device of rotoscoping, creating animated images using frames of live-action footage as patterns. Rotoscoping has been used to integrate qualities of filmic and animated representation in many other animated features as well as in some computer programs [see, for instance, *The Halley Project* (Mindscape) and *McGraw-Hill Math Courseware* created by Tom Snyder Productions].

The second integration technique mentioned above—creating a context in which different media can comfortably coexist—is illustrated by the *NewSpeek* system developed at the MIT Media Laboratory (see Color Plate VIII). *NewSpeek* assembles news information items on the basis of a person's stated interests and preferences and presents them in the context of a newspaper with "illustrations" that may be motion video (a similar technique was used in the Movie Manual project, also at the Media Lab). Dynamic documents, talking books, and animated icons all employ context as a means of integrating diverse media. Media integration can also be enhanced by providing uniform means for people to manipulate and control objects of different media types. The topic of media integration will be treated further in the section on multimedia in Chapter 6.

## Symmetry in Representation

Symmetry is a kind of pattern. As discussed in Chapter 2, we derive pleasure from patterns in representations, and we also sometimes expect certain kinds of patterns to occur. Although there are many reasons for emphasizing one modality over another, we tend to expect that the modalities involved in a representation will have roughly the same "resolution." A simplistic cartoon-style animation with naturalistic character voices and environment sounds, for instance, seems out of whack. A computer game that incorporates breathtakingly high-resolution, high-speed animation but only produces little beeps seems brain-damaged.

We also tend to expect symmetry between the input and output modalities of a system; that is, we expect that they are operating in the same sensory universe as the rest of the representation. If a computer talks to us, we want to be able to talk back, and vice versa. If we can push on a part of the system, we would probably like, or even expect, the system to push back—this is the key to the effectiveness of force-feedback controllers. In most systems, our side of the I/O equation is severely impoverished. The system can present images, sounds, movements, words, and possibly even speech, but we must act inside a straitjacket of menu items and mouse clicks. No wonder we often feel that computers are always in control—the system is holding all the cards! Working toward symmetry in input and output channels in human-computer activities can vastly improve our experience of engagement and agency.

This chapter has presented several rules of thumb pertaining to the design of the various elements in a dramatic representation. Many of those principles have appeared in different forms in the literature of human factors and interface design, and many are simply intuitive. By incorporating them into an overarching notion of interactive representation, we have attempted to deepen our understanding of the derivation of such rules and the relationships among them. The final chapter of this book is devoted to applying these principles to some key areas in human-computer activity.

Chapter Six

# New Directions in Human-Computer Activity

## Building a Better Mousetrap

Reviewers and critics of my work have often asked me to provide examples of how dramatic theory can be used to improve existing products and applications. In response, I have incorporated examples of "dramatic successes" into the earlier sections of this book, pointing out effective uses of direct-manipulation techniques, the creation of virtualities, the use of agents, and the integration of multiple modalities in representations.

Reviewers have also commented that my examples are often drawn from the domain of computer games. It should be noted that I am not an avid game player. I find most computer games to be boring, frustrating, and "obstructionist" in the sense that they require players to solve puzzles primarily for the purpose of extending the duration of game play. I also abhor the violent content that is characteristic of mainstream computer games. But I must observe that computer games (including arcade games, videogames, and PC games) have been the principal means whereby most people in the world have come into contact with computers for the first time (although bank teller machines are probably a close second). As game designer and researcher Chris Crawford [1990] observes, computer games have often been in the forefront of "friendly" interface design, being the first consumer computer applications to employ such techniques as multisensory representation, kinesthetic input and tight coupling of kinesthetic and visual modalities, speech and other auditory output, and first-person visual point of view.

A challenge that I have set for myself throughout the writing of this book is to think about using these theories to build a better mousetrap, perhaps in the form of a word processor. I keep coming up against the same problem: Since it is true that interface and application are (or should be) the same context, and since it is true that the interfaces to existing applications reflect not only the interface design but also the conception of the application itself, it is difficult to improve the interface without reconceptualizing the whole action. In fact, that is exactly what needs to be done in most cases.

We need to remember the evolutionary history of computer applications. They began with the notion of computers as calculation devices, followed shortly by the notion of computers as tools for text entry and editing, first in the context of programming and later in the context of other types of written documents. Then it was discovered that we could draw and make music with them. Applications have been mapped onto these specific activities in a tool-like way. This *recapitulation* of previous forms and activities is an entirely natural and necessary process in the evolution of all media, as we will discuss further in the section on virtual reality at the end of this chapter.

However, tool-like applications that focus narrowly on known sorts of tasks tend to break up our experience of doing things. The current state of document creation with computers is a case in point, where a person may use a database manager, an outline processor, a word processor, drawing and painting programs, and a page layout program either alternately or serially in the preparation of some single thing—that is, in the performance of what should be an integrated, whole action.

As current research and development into integrated document creation implies, a new evolutionary force is entering the picture in the development of the computer medium: new *visions* of constellations of activities that must be considered together if we are to afford people the satisfaction of participating in *whole actions* that are of the same magnitude as the goals that drive their component activities. Like Ted Nelson's notion of virtuality, such integrated environments present the possibility of doing things that we simply couldn't do before. Imagine, for instance, what it would be like if the process of *writing* were a fluid, natural, and unified activity.

## An Environment for Writing

In his paper entitled "Cognitive Artifacts," Donald Norman describes the way in which certain artifacts can make us appear to be smarter. He defines cognitive artifacts as "those artificial devices that maintain, display, or operate upon information in order to serve a representational function and that affect human cognitive performance." [Norman, 1990] He uses the example of a preflight checklist to be used by airline pilots to check out a plane's safety features before take-off. Norman's point is that, although from the outside view the checklist makes pilots appear to be "smarter" in that it improves their performance in checking safety features, what is going on from the person's perspective is that the artifact has *changed the nature of the task*. Now instead of having to remember, think about, and investigate all of the plane's safety features, the pilot's task is to read items on a checklist and perform a set of prescribed actions.

It seems obvious to me that Norman's principle is reversible; that is, while new cognitive artifacts can change the nature of tasks, it is also true that new understandings of tasks can (or should) effect changes in the design of cognitive artifacts. A new vision of the task changes what the artifact needs to be. We may not be able to make significant improvements in word processors or spreadsheets. But by using this permutation of the theory of cognitive artifacts, we might define tasks differently and cluster them together so as to envision more holistic and complete representational environments, contexts, and actions. The task of writing has already been transformed by the computer to include visual as well as textual information—for instance, visual elements can be integrated more easily with computers than they could be in the days of typewriters.

To explore the activity of writing further, I reflected first on my experiences with my word processor. I hated Microsoft Word 4.0 at first because there was so much to learn, because it was so hard to learn it (the product supported discovery-style learning poorly and the manual seemed to be organized not around the actions that I might want to perform but rather around the product's "features"), and because many of the new features seemed to conflict with things I had learned about other word processors (most notably, Microsoft Word 1.0 and 3.0). So I learned what I could by doing things and asking people for help. At some point after about two weeks of intentional learning, I reached my limit.

At that point, I made a compromise with Word: I don't use all of it; it gets me by and it doesn't pull any funny business. I discovered upon reflection that the parts of the program that I actually use most effectively fall into two categories: the direct-manipulation features and the familiar or conventional features. Using my own experience to create a specification for redesigning the representation, I came up with these criteria:

1. Direct-manipulation characteristics: Whenever possible, transform specification activities into direct-manipulation ones. For example, most of the items in the format and document menus could be represented graphically with the ability to resize, reshape, and relocate visual elements. The successes in the current version of the product are distinct but isolated: The icons on the "ruler" that represent tabs and line spacing, the "borders" construction facility, and the "page view" facility.

2. Familiar and conventional features:
   a. Take advantage of things that are familiar from the past: Subtracting those direct-manipulation elements that were easy to learn in the first place, I'm left with some concepts that have become part of the concept of word processing in some deep sense: the idea of a document, the idea of editing text, the idea of designing the document's appearance. Other familiar elements, like document formatting conventions and the use of outlining, come from precomputer days. All of these are elements of the evolving mythos of the activity.
   b. Take advantage of things that are familiar from the larger context: For example, thanks to the *Apple Human Interface Guidelines* [1987], certain interface features and characteristics like "cut," "paste," and "copy" are practically universal in Macintosh applications, including the Finder (which is commonly perceived as the "system," rather than another application). On the Macintosh as well as on other hardware platforms, overlapping subsets of identical tools or functions in related applications (such as drawing, painting, or drafting) are represented identically at the interface. Consistency with these larger worlds extends the range of the activity not only in terms of its subtasks but in terms of the representational context. The sense of working in this larger context begins to replace the notion of applications with a notion of activities that transcend conventional application boundaries. It also suggests that *the granularity of "applications" is too small.*

What kind of representation would support a larger view of the activity of writing? Work is proceeding in many hardware and software companies to create integrated applications environments where the boundaries of various applications can be crossed with minimal disruption and context-shifting. However, creating an environment for writing that consists of a fixed set of integrated applications may still not provide optimal flexibility and scope in the definition of the whole action. How do we determine the proper cluster of activities (or applications) that constitute an environment for document creation? We can identify three dimensions that describe the activity space:

1. The dimension of applications: For any given person involved in a particular writing activity, this dimension might include idea processing; information retrieval and database management; the making, storing, and editing of images; performing calculations; importing data from other applications; and document design.
2. The dimension of activities: This dimension might include finding and integrating resource materials, entering and editing text, selecting and designing visual representations, developing ideas (by working on their expression), or working in a particular genre (fiction versus research papers, for instance). Notice that this activity map does not correspond neatly to the way that the set of conventional applications carves up the world.
3. The dimension of goals and purposes: Various goals include self-expression, document creation as an aid to thinking, sketching out ideas (making a first draft), or creating a final presentation to communicate with an intended audience.

How can we draw a fixed circle around any part of that three-dimensional landscape? A dramatic view suggests that we draw the circle *dynamically*, according to an understanding of the action. A system that can capture the dimension of activities and the dimension of goals and purposes, through either implicit or explicit means, could enable us to dynamically construct appropriate contexts for the action as it unfolds. New contexts could be created as the person's focus changes, like different scenes in the same play or rooms in the same house. In this sense, the designer's role is transformed from the creation and integration of applications (and interfaces) to the creation of environments, objects with appropriate affordances [Norman, 1988], and characters appropriate to the action (agents).

How does this approach affect the shape of the whole action? In the segmented, applications-style approach, the shape of the action tends to "flatline." In terms of the Freytag graph, the action involved in isolated tasks like information retrieval and text editing does not possess enough *significance* to yield a line that deviates much from the horizontal. These activities are undertaken for the sake of a larger goal, and as part of a larger action. Isolated tasks must be contextualized into meaningful realms of activity—as parts of an action that is large enough to be pleasurable. By taking action in integrated and dynamic representational contexts, a person is better able to sense the shape of the whole and the relationship of each component activity to the larger action. If the action is defined in sufficient magnitude, the steps toward its accomplishment are transformed from flatline segments to a recognizable variation of the characteristic Freytag curve.

Computers have the potential to transform the process of writing from a series of isolated and cumbersome tasks into a whole action that retains and refreshes its connections to its inspiration, materials, and outcome. By designing writing environments that unify the process, writing can be represented as an action that constantly reflects its purpose and significance.

## *The Smart House: Actions in Search of Characters*

My family is full of computer junkies. There are four Macintosh computers at home. Two of them are in the study, where they function as workstations for my husband and me. One is in the kitchen, as part of an ongoing project of mine to figure out what on earth it might be good for there. I use it to store recipes, create menu plans and grocery lists, maintain accounting of household expenses, write poetry and personal correspondence, and do other miscellaneous personal and domestic things like designing coloring books and party invitations for my kids.[1] The fourth Mac is in the kids' room, where the two of them (ages two and five at this writing) use an alphabet program their daddy wrote for them and play with other learning games.

There are numerous other microprocessors in my house that aren't living in Macintoshes. There is a programmable thermostat with a digital display. There are microprocessors in the TV, alarm clock, food processor, VCR, stereo, answering machine, calculator, washer and dryer, dishwasher, oven, various electronic toys, and many other devices. Other things in our household respond to us and our environment in various "smart" ways—the outside lights turn on when something stalks through the driveway, the garage light turns on when I open the garage door, and the walkway lights turn on when it gets dark. The question is, why don't all the great electronic and microprocessor-based gadgets we have or might have in our homes *talk* to each other? Who are these guys, anyway, and why can't I get them to cooperate?

The National Association of Homebuilders has recently removed the primary technical stumbling block to integration of the various "smart" devices in homes by agreeing on a standard for transmitting data and controlling electrical devices in various ways. They have developed standards for three kinds of cables: electric power with data, gas with data, and communications with data. In the future, new homes will be "wired" with these capabilities, setting the stage for the technological possibility of integrating the distributed "intelligence" in our homes [see Sussman, 1988].

There are obvious advantages to organizing all the distributed intelligence in my house into a single system through

---

[1]Using computers to store recipes is one of the oldest jokes in the personal computer business—in the early days, that's what all marketing executives thought women would do with them. The obvious drawback is that cookie dough, pasta sauce, and other goo-based substances will get all over the keys when you try to retrieve a recipe file. A speech interface is the obvious solution, but it would seem that the marketing executives haven't thought of that one yet. I wonder how many of them cook.

which their actions can be controlled and their interactions orchestrated. The functions of various appliances and systems are highly interrelated in various contexts—the context of vacations, for instance. When I leave home, I want to turn the thermostat down, turn the water heater down, arrange for certain lights to come on (so as to create the illusion of being at home), figure out how to get my plants watered, turn on the security system, activate the automatic forwarding program on my telephone answering machine and my various e-mail systems. I also want to figure out how to feed the cat and I want the furnace and water heater to warm things up a few hours before I get home. How lovely it would be to dial up a vacation plan and have it automatically executed every time the family is away. Of course, the winter plan wouldn't work in the summer, and I might not want things to "power down" as completely during a two-day absence as a two-week trip. How lovely it would be if I could use my computer to create and tailor plans and to manage their execution.

For this and many other contexts (entertainment and entertaining, for example, or the cluster of activities centered around food), centralization of control and orchestration of functionality would be a dream come true—the dream of a smart house.[2] Nicholas Negroponte, director of the MIT Media Laboratory, envisions smart environments populated with agents:

> Direct manipulation has its place, and in many regards is part of the joys of life: sports, food, sex, and for some, driving. But wouldn't you really prefer to run your home and office life with a gaggle of well trained butlers (to answer the telephone), maids (to make the hospital corners), secretaries (to filter the world), accountants or brokers (to manage your money),[3] and on some occasions, cooks, gardeners, and chauffeurs when

---

[2]Of course, one can imagine many ways in which a not-so-smart house can go horribly wrong. Ray Bradbury has described two of them in his stories, "The Murderer," in which a man murders his smart house, and "The Veldt," in which children feed their parents to a pack of virtual lions they conjured up in their interactive rec room.

[3]Negroponte adds, "This one might make you nervous."

> there were too many guests, weeds, or cars on the road? [Negroponte, 1990]

Whether the smart house should consist of one agent (as in some of Ray Bradbury's stories) or many (as in Negroponte's vision) is an interesting question. The contexts and functions of a smart house would seem to require many and varied kinds of knowledge and skill. They also suggest a variety of different emotional characteristics and values. Accountants and gardeners behave differently, and interactions with them evoke different moods and emotional responses. The smart house as a single character combining all of the necessary traits would be omnimorphous and omnipotent in ways that could be uncomfortable, perhaps even menacing (a sort of Big Brother at home). In Japan, a unified approach has been taken with a model smart house called the TRON (standing for The Real-time Operating-system Nucleus) house. Here are some of its features:

> Sensors in the roof and computers in the walls, for example, automatically open and close the windows to maintain optimum ventilation. If the telephone rings while you are listening to music, the volume is automatically reduced. The toilet notes the user's pulse and blood pressure and analyzes urine for sugar and protein levels, providing a daily health checkup. . . . Much of the guesswork has been taken out of cooking. Recipes are put in the kitchen computer. A flip of a switch adds the appropriate amount of seasoning to the nearest milligram. [Sado, 1990]

To an individualistic American, the TRON house might take on the persona of a demented Nurse Ratchet, denying permission to open the windows for a blast of cold air, invading the privacy of the body, and insisting on the preparation of unvarying hospital food.

Breaking the system up into multiple agents that have knowledge about each others' goals and actions would seem to be the better solution. Such a system would employ agents and contexts that are similar to those in the real world, giving people a "leg up" in working with them. The multiple agents solution also allows more efficient use of context-specific verbal and gestural "vocabularies." But why not define the multiple agents as the devices themselves, giving people direct control over their various operations? The answer is twofold: the desire to incorporate task- and context-specific expertise in the system (which would usually require the orchestration of multiple devices and functions), and the comfortable magnitude and emotional tractability of the characters.

If Negroponte's list can be taken as at least a partial cast of characters (one might add a house-sitter, for instance), then what is the plot? Can all of the discrete transactions with the various agents in the system be seen to form something like a whole action? The title of this section is drawn from a twentieth-century play by Luigi Pirandello, *Six Characters in Search of an Author*, in which six characters with complex traits and relationships approach a playwright with the request that he write them a script that will let them exercise their dramatic potential. What is the play that is performed by all the agents in the smart house? Negroponte suggests an answer: "The stage is set with characters of your own choice or creation whose scripts are drawn from the *play of your life*" (italics mine) [Negroponte, 1990].

After all, a primary characteristic of dramatic form is a certain basic simplification of life. Causal connections are less obscure. There is less randomness and "noise" in the system. The overall action, even with its crises and reversals, has a pleasing shape. These are just the sorts of qualities we strive for in managing the exigencies of everyday life. We certainly don't want our lives to be reduced to daily episodes of a soap opera, but it would be comforting if our agents could make the daily hassles of running a household into something more like episodes in a little ongoing "series" of their own—a series in which every episode provides catharsis and we are regular guest stars.

# Multimedia

Multimedia (a word that, for some of us, evokes unfortunate associations with big, black Bell and Howell projectors and boring "educational" filmstrips) now refers to systems that deliver more than text and graphics in their visual displays (typically, photographic images, audio, or video) and which characteristically utilize some kind of computer and some kind of optical storage medium. Currently, their primary use is in applications built around the storage and retrieval of information in a variety of media types. Multimedia systems have been created for applications in education, training, work-related task aids, and entertainment. After a few false starts in the 1980s, multimedia now seems likely to become a new "fixture" of our media environment in this decade, if the near-term hurdles of warring hardware platforms and data formats can be cleared. Multimedia systems and the experiences they deliver may have as great an impact on our culture as computer games, movies, or even television. Given this potential, it seems appropriate to look at some of the cultural issues that arise and to think about ways in which a dramatic approach might help us address them. Among the key cultural (and some would say political) issues are the content, validity, and accessibility of information.

Thanks to the "form" of the television docudrama, it seems oxymoronic to many to think about using dramatic means to represent information. "Drama" is the part of docudrama that means it's a lie—that is, the literal truth has been reshaped to the end of elucidation, "higher truth," or, most likely, entertainment revenue. "Dramatic re-enactment" is a related television phenomenon, disguised as the representation of information, but actually intended, one suspects, to boost the ratings of the nightly news. The problem in these cases is that the truthfulness or accuracy of information is apparently compromised for reasons that may be less than honorable, and the tool in the hand of the devil seems to be dramatic form. In the Guides project, for instance, user testing of the first video prototype version revealed what we might term a "docudrama bias." Some people stated explicitly that, because the video segments looked like TV, the information contained in them was suspect. Many judged text-based materials, most of which were drawn from *Grolier's Encyclopedia America*, as more truthful and informative than information presented in the video medium [see Karimi et al., 1989, and Laurel et al., 1990]. In the television age, seeing is no longer believing.[4]

Before discussing how the project team for the current version of Guides (Tim Oren, Abbe Don, and myself) addressed this issue, it is worthwhile to review one of the goals of the project as it evolved through the various prototypes. We suspected that new forms of information would eventually lead to a new kind of "information literacy." We noted that central components of information are its source and point of view. One of the problems with docudrama, for instance, is that we don't know whose axe is being ground in the selection, arrangement, and sometimes invention of materials. Docudrama makes a claim to objectivity, but it is too easy to see how political, philosophical, and expedient concerns could come into play in the reshaping of information. Furthermore, we observed that "objectivity" itself is popularly misunderstood; that is, in our society, objectivity is confused with the *absence* of point of view. In most cases, such as history textbooks or evening news broadcasts, objectivity actually is bound by the invisible workings of a decidedly Western worldview and set of values. Just as speakers of a regional dialect often think that everyone but themselves has an accent, mainstream participants of a culture seem to believe that everyone but themselves has an attitude.

The premise of the design team was that point of view is always present in information, because information always reflects something about its source and its purpose. Information is a kind of representation, a made thing, that is influenced by its efficient, formal, material, and end causes.

---

[4]Parts of this section were presented in a panel on multimedia interfaces at CHI '90.

Our belief was that a desirable component of information literacy would be the ability to identify and understand point of view as a dimension of any information that one might encounter, so as to weigh, judge, or interpret the information accordingly. We then set about determining what were the outward and visible signs of point of view that we could employ to make it more salient. One is the material provided by the object of the information. Another is the character of the source—the traits, values, goals, and context of the agent who created the information. A third indicator of point of view is the relationship of the information to its source as implied by its *form*—is the information a first-person account of an experience, hearsay, or a hypothetical scenario?

In an attempt to make use of these indicators in the multimedia representation, we created three agent characters —guides—to embody three alternative points of view about the various topics in American history that were treated in the database: a frontiersman, a Native American, and a settler woman. Abbe Don, who conceived of and implemented the first "video guide," collected first-person accounts of incidents and topics related to westward expansion in America from diaries and journals to serve as materials for the three new guides. We cast three performers (a storyteller, a novelist, and an anthropologist, as it turned out) to perform these stories in a video format. The stories then became part of the database, associated with many of the same topics that were covered in the encyclopedia articles that made up the bulk of the database content.

In an attempt to address the problems of credibility of video materials that were raised in user testing of the second prototype, we decided to retain some of the features of the former version and modify others. We were resolved to retain character (in the form of anthropomorphic agents) to represent the source of information and to provide context, and we began searching for other hypotheses to explain the "docudrama bias." We noted that in the user-testing version the guide told stories in various natural settings, and we reasoned that this "production value" tended to make the video segments seem more like little docudramas than stories, and so we resolved to eliminate this element by shooting the new versions as "talking heads" in a studio against a neutral backdrop. We suspected that the docudrama effect might also have been exacerbated by the fact that the video sequences appeared on a separate monitor that was identical to a TV screen, while the textual information was displayed by the "objective" computer [see Don, 1990]. To combat this effect, we integrated the video display into the computer screen.

Finally, we noted that the user-testing prototype did not give enough direct information about the sources of the various first-person materials, so we designed an introductory video segment in which the performers introduced themselves and described their real-life professions, gave the names of the people whose journals were used as source materials, and talked a bit about what they had learned about the lives, experiences, and values of such people. This "Brechtian" element was designed to establish the roles of the agents as *storytellers* rather than fictitious characters, thereby reinforcing their credibility. (Color Plate IX).

The docudrama bias is but one of many media biases that are present in our culture. For instance, information represented as text is generally judged by members of our culture to be more truthful and contentful than information presented orally [see Ong, 1982, and Don, 1990]. One goal in the shaping of a new information literacy is to replace these biases with more productive understandings of the powers and limitations of various media. Perhaps the most direct way to accomplish this goal is to provide multiple representations of information in different media, so that people can observe the differences themselves. An oral story performance, for instance, provides channels of information that are not offered by text, including paralinguistic variables like inflection, pitch, and pace in speech, gestures, and other aspects of physical enactment. The differences could be emphasized in an activity that involved information presented in one of these "ancillary" oral channels as a key component.

A complementary goal is to integrate various media so that the experience of information in a multimedia system can be organic rather than compartmentalized. In the Guides project we pursued this goal in four ways:

1. We established greater parity in the quantity of information of different media types in the database.
2. We added the ability to "link" information of different media types (cross-media links).
3. We designed a universal set of controls for examining information of different media types, which required that we employ a notion of granularity for each medium that was roughly symmetrical.
4. Finally, we employed a narrative rather than a navigational approach to information retrieval.

The first three points have been discussed in Chapters 1 and 5 [see Laurel et al., 1990, for more detailed information]. Don provides a description of the narrative approach:

> Narrative includes both the story being told (content) and the conditions of its telling (structure and context). Similarly, creating a multimedia knowledgebase involves selecting or generating information as well as representing the structure and the content to the user through the interface. All too often, these activities occur separately. A narrative approach to multimedia interface design provides a framework that allows the structure and content of the knowledgebase to evolve together while accommodating a variety of contexts defined by the user's needs and interests. Within that framework, interface designers can adopt strategies from narrative theory, such as including multiple representations of events and information, or using characters as a means of representing material with an explicitly acknowledged point of view [Don, 1990].

In the Guides project the typical spatial metaphor employed in most hypertext or hypermedia databases is replaced by the notion of information, not as a space, but as *a series of events unfolding over time*. People do not "navigate to" information; rather information comes to them from a variety of sources. Besides storytelling, the other principal function of the guides is to make suggestions about what one might want to look at next in the database, based on each guide's point of view and the information that is currently being displayed. A guide's point of view is represented by an information-retrieval algorithm that associates the guide more or less strongly with various topics and information items in the database. To take a guide's suggestion, a person need only click on its title (as displayed in the guide's "suggestion box") and the selected item will appear. In addition to the three historical guides, the system also includes a *frame guide* whose point of view is roughly equivalent to that of a reference librarian, and whose suggestions for next items are based purely on topical proximity to the current selection. The system also includes the facility for people to construct *custom guides* with their own unique topical interests and media preferences. Thus at any given moment, people may have as many as five suggestions that they can take, as well as access to an instrumental searching facility that enables direct searching of the database by title or topic. By using the guides' suggestions, the action unfolds much like an elaborate story created by one or more characters in collaboration with the human agent.

Of course, there are critical differences between such a narrative experience and a dramatic one. For example, an experience with Guides is likely to exhibit narrative extensification rather than dramatic intensification because of the existence of multiple representations and the availability and seductiveness of side-trips and midcourse adjustments. But Guides has features that are dramatic as well. Agents (including people) take action in a representational context. There are clear causal relations between actions and the traits of their agents. The information itself is not enacted (except for the video stories), but the actions of *seeking* and *examining* information are. The whole action is shaped by the choices and actions of the various characters. One might imagine an information-retrieval system at the dramatic end of the continuum, where informational *content* is enacted in dramatic form. Such an experience may await "through the looking glass"[5] in the world of virtual reality. The issues of credibility and point of view may be even more deeply embedded in systems that are designed to provide immersive experiences for people in virtual worlds.

## Virtual Reality

At NASA, Autodesk, and VPL Research, demos of "virtual reality" start out innocently enough, once you get through putting on all the gear—eyephones with stereoscopic displays and a glove or suit with position-sensing equipment, all cabled up to receivers. Through the eyephones you will probably see a relatively low-resolution 3-D graphics version of an office, like the one you're actually standing in (Color Plate X). As you move your head, you can look around the office (although, if the frame rate is too slow, you'll probably feel a little bit of "simulator sickness"). You can see a representation of your hand as you reach for a book on the shelf; your virtual hand may either grab the book or slide through it like the hand of a ghost. Then maybe you'll stumble upon a gesture that points up (or somebody will suggest it to you) and—*whoa!*—you fly above the office, higher and higher, until it's just a little construct far below, and you are surrounded by the darkness of cyberspace.

Then they'll start giving you the sexier demos. At NASA you can fly through a model of the space shuttle. As you approach the bulkhead at breakneck speed, you'll probably feel your muscles tense for the impact, and when you melt through it as if it wasn't there (which of course it isn't), you'll feel a physical adrenaline rush. At VPL, you may enter a *Reality Built for Two* and interact with the animated body of another person who's hooked into your virtual world, either

---

[5]This allusion was coined by John Walker, president and founder of Autodesk, Inc., in the context of Autodesk's virtual-reality system.

in the same physical room or across the globe (Color Plate V, the illustration for *Habitat* in Chapter 5).

As you fly around these imaginary spaces, you may experience, as I did, a few little cognitive train wrecks. In the NASA system, one flies by pointing—specific gestures control the direction of movement. What if you fly past the shuttle and want to turn around and fly back? Do you just physically turn around? Sure enough, there's the shuttle back behind you. Or you can make your flying-pointing gesture back over your shoulder, in which case you might fly backwards and upside down. The claim is made that virtual reality is just like reality itself, but as this case illustrates, it's like reality only different.

## Some Holes in the Paradigm

The development of virtual-reality systems can be traced back at least as far as Ivan Sutherland's *Sketchpad*, and much farther in fiction and fantasy. Its current instantiation, employing a head-mounted display environment, is probably most directly attributable to the work of Scott S. Fisher at the MIT Media Laboratory, Atari Systems Research, and NASA Ames Research [see Fisher, 1990]. Major American players include NASA, Autodesk, VPL Research, Dr. Fred Brooks' laboratory at the University of North Carolina, and the new human interface lab at the University of Washington under the direction of former Air Force researcher Tom Furness. The notion of virtual reality has been enhanced by the fiction of William Gibson (inventor of "cyberspace") and other writers in the Cyberpunk genre, as well as the Holodeck construct developed by the creators of *Star Trek: The Next Generation*. Information on virtual reality can also be found in Fisher [1990], Rheingold [1990], and Krueger [1990]. For a complete review of the virtual-reality phenomenon, see Howard Rheingold's *Virtual Reality*, [forthcoming].

In an article entitled "Through the Looking Glass," Autodesk founder John Walker describes the promise of virtual reality:

> Now we're at the threshold of the next revolution in user-computer interaction: a technology that will take the user through the screen into the world "inside" the computer—a world in which the user can interact with three-dimensional objects whose fidelity will grow as computing power increases and display technology progresses. This virtual world can be whatever the designer makes it. As designers and users explore entirely new experiences and modes of interaction, they will be jointly defining the next generation of user interaction with computers [Walker, 1990].

With demo-able systems to provide the initial conversion experience, virtual reality is making a huge impact on our hopes and expectations about the experiential qualities of tomorrow's human-computer activities. Yet it seems that there are some rather serious obstacles to be overcome before virtual reality can deliver the robust kinds of experiences that we fantasize about. Some of the "old" problems that faced us when we were designing human-computer activities without eyephones remain: How do people and systems understand each other? How can the actions of both be shaped and orchestrated?

Jaron Lanier, founder of VPL, attempts to obviate what appear to be some of the central challenges in the construction of virtual worlds:

> Let's suppose that you could have a time machine go back to the earliest creatures who developed language, our ancestors at some point, and give them Virtual Reality clothing. Would they have developed language? I suspect not, because as soon as you can change the world in any way, that is a mode of expression of utter power and eloquence; it makes description seem a bit limited. . . . [The idea of] post-symbolic communication . . . means that when you're able to improvise reality as you can in Virtual Reality, and when that's shared with other people, you don't really need to describe the world any more because you can simply make any contingency. You don't really need to describe an action because you can create any action [Lanier interview in Heilbrun, 1989].

I have two problems with the view represented by Lanier's comments. One is that language is good for more than describing the physical world. The ability to create and manipulate symbolic representations is probably the central feature of human intelligence and imagination. It also expedites the process of human communication (do I have to paint you a picture?). Alas, the hard problem of language understanding (and the deeper forms of inference that must go along with it in intelligent systems) just won't go away with the wave of a DataGlove.

A deeper objection is to the glossing over of the problems of designing action. Yes, I can do "anything" in a virtual world, but how does the world respond? According to what principles? And if there are computer-based as well as human agents in the world (Captain Kirk, for example, or Adam Selene), how would they be constructed and represented? What would constitute their "intelligence"? The rhetoric around virtual reality reminds me of the rhetoric around interactive movies a few years ago, when people (including some Very Important Film People) talked about them as if they would just *happen*, like the reverse of *The Purple Rose of Cairo*. One day you would just get up out of your theatre seat and walk right into the screen and then—well then, interesting things would happen.

The notion of virtual reality is a continuum that is older even than science fiction. Enactments around prehistoric campfires, Greek theatre, and performance rituals of aboriginal people the world over are all aimed at the same goal: Heightened experience through multisensory representation. *Sketchpad*, *Pong*, and cyberspace are all stops on the same route. Myron Krueger's groundbreaking work on VIDEOPLACE and other video-based interactive environments, as well as many of the "media room" projects developed at the MIT Media Laboratory, demonstrate other approaches to the creation of mimetic environments with sensory richness [see Krueger, 1990, and Laurel, 1986a, for descriptions of these projects]. What we have in today's virtual-reality systems is the confluence of three very powerful enactment capabilities: sensory immersion, remote presence, and tele-operations. These capabilities do indeed hold enormous promise, but they will not make the central challenge go away—that is, *designing and orchestrating action in virtual worlds.*

Part of the virtual-reality finesse is the technique of plugging other humans into the system as the other agents in an action. But even when the system is responsible for maintaining no agents *per se,* it is still the case that the kinds of actions that can occur are constrained by the affordances of the world—the material aspects of the representation. If those materials are as fluidly changeable as Lanier's description suggests, then there is the additional problem of establishing common ground among human agents who share the virtual environment. Finally, there is the comparatively quaint problem of giving the action a pleasing shape. A belief in the powers of form in representations seems to be orthogonal to the kind of imaginative free-fall that many virtual reality pundits envision.

The virtual reality community must eventually welcome these prodigal problems back home. It is not enough to be able to look at the backside of a computer graphic, or even to walk or fly around a virtual environment of extreme complexity and multisensory detail. I can imagine a virtual haunted house, for instance, with boards creaking, curtains waving, rats scurrying, and strange smells wafting from the basement. Sooner or later, something will have to *happen,* and if it does, that something will be interpreted (at least by my dramatically predisposed brain) to be the beginning of an unfolding plot.

## Beyond the Yellow Brick Road

In the School of Computer Science at Carnegie Mellon University, Joseph Bates' Oz group is working on the "backend" of virtual reality—using AI technology to generate interesting plots and characters on the fly in collaboration with first-person, real-time "interactors." An overarching goal is to create robustly interactive imaginary worlds that are predisposed to yield *dramatic* experiences in both formal and emotional terms. "Robust interactivity" means that a user's choices and actions have a significant influence on the evolving plot. The Oz group identifies their domain as interactive fiction, and their work is focused in three areas:

- Autonomous computer-based agents (that could serve as characters in imaginary worlds)
- Pragmatics-based natural language generation (to generate dialogue and/or narrative text)
- Applying dramatic theory to the problem of interactive plot generation

I have been working with the Oz team on capturing both theoretical and performance-oriented dimensions of dramatic expertise.

## Mediated Improvisations

In the spring of 1990 the Oz team, in collaboration with the Drama Department at Carnegie Mellon, conducted a series of technologically mediated dramatic improvisations to investigate the range and effectiveness of various dramatic techniques in shaping interactive plots in real time. I developed the form of the experiment at the Atari Systems Research Laboratory in 1984, in collaboration with Scott Fisher, other then-Atari researchers, and novelist Ray Bradbury. The Atari lab was closed before we were able to do a complete run, but the baton has been successfully passed to Oz. The improv at Carnegie Mellon involved three actors, a director, a scenarist, a videographer, and a "naive" person who served as the interactor. The actors and director were used to simulate corresponding components of a computer-based interactive fantasy system. The effectiveness of the emerging plot was judged in terms of both its "objective" formal and structural elements and the experience of the interactor.

The scenarist (Margaret Kelso of the Carnegie Mellon Drama Department), working from an idea of what would constitute a powerful experience for the interactor, began with the desired climax, planning backward from it to visualize alternative contributory incidents, and working forward toward it in real time as the plot was constructed. A director who specialized in theatrical improvisation was given the scenario in the form of a plot graph. The actors wore headsets through which they could receive audio transmissions from a director who viewed the action from backstage. The entire experiment was videotaped for further analysis.[6] Each of the three actors were given information about the locale (a bus station), few salient character traits, and one or more character goals. The actors began improvising a scene on the basis of that information.

The interactor was also given information about the locale and the single goal of buying a bus ticket to attend the funeral of a relative in another city. A short while after the scene began, the interactor entered the imaginary world. As the action unfolded, the director consulted the plot graph and drew upon her own dramatic expertise to make suggestions to the actors through their headsets. She employed a variety of techniques, including goal intensification, statements of salience, and explicitly theatrical, performance-oriented directives. All of her directions to the actors were intended to contribute to the creation of a dramatically satisfying plot that incorporated the unconstrained choices of the interactor. Two improvisations were conducted with two different interactors.

The results were powerful, in terms of both the lessons learned about kinds of knowledge needed to synthesize plot interactively and the level of engagement and catharsis experienced by the interactors. The experiment led to several discoveries:

- The "third eye" of the remote director was a key factor in the satisfactory shaping of the whole.

---

[6]We noted that, because there was live video, the director could in fact have worked from a remote location—an idea that we intend to pursue in future versions.

- The knowledge required of the actors and director spanned both the domain of the imaginary world and the domain of dramatic theory and performance. Specific kinds of complementarity between directors" and performers' knowledge were observed.
- The interactor experienced time quite differently than the other observers of the action. Commonalities were observed in the dramatic structure of the most radically time-distorted events.
- Mediated improvisations are not performance pieces in the traditional sense. As theatre viewed from the outside, the entertainment value of the improvisations was largely mediocre. In contrast, the interactors' experiences were dramatically quite powerful.
- The engaging aspect of viewing mediated improvisations is not their theatrical finesse, but rather the experience of watching the real-time sculpting of the plot by the director and actors in response to the interactor's choices and actions.

## The Future of Mediated Improvisation

In addition to their uses in revealing and clarifying ways in which dramatic expertise can be embedded in the architecture of interactive fantasy systems, mediated improvs can make important contributions at the other end of the spectrum: the virtual-reality interface.

In collaboration with Scott Fisher, I have sketched out several possible permutations of mediated improv, not only as a means for learning about interactive drama but also as a way of viewing the process of real-time "action sculpture." A near-term project is for a public installation using essentially the same format as the Carnegie Mellon experiment but with a larger role for video. In the installation version, interested viewers can watch improvs via video with the director's audio channel superimposed. By mounting tiny cameras on the actors' and interactors' headsets, we can allow the director and other viewers to look into the action from the point of view of any character.[7] Guest scenarists and directors can be invited to participate. For multilingual audiences, viewers can be offered simultaneous translations of the director's audio and the performance dialogue in various languages.

A more elaborate version boosts the technological gain again by giving the actors and interactor virtual bodies in virtual environments. In this version, all participants experience the action via a first-person virtual-reality interface. The participants' virtual bodies are choreographed directly through kinesthetic input. Speech and voice qualities may be technologically altered in real time to suit character. The director is still a voice in the actors' heads, but he or she may also influence the action by manipulating mood, atmosphere, and situation through direct access to scenic elements and virtual objects.

A long-term goal is to devise a version of mediated improv that can serve as a "frontend" to the Oz system. In this version, characters may be enacted, not by people, but by Oz software. Only the interactors are humans participating in real time. The director becomes a real-time programmer that eventually merges into the system itself. In this way, our work with mediated improvs can intersect with the Oz project to create a robust, multisensory interactive fantasy system.

## A New Opposable Thumb

A unique and wonderful characteristic of the medium of virtual reality is the discourse surrounding it. The conversation is very broad and rich, involving people from technology, the arts, social sciences, and philosophy. It encourages a fusion of these concerns in a way of thinking among its participants. Also unique is the fact that many of those participants have communication skills that allow them to speak directly about

[7]The use of multiple POV video channels begins to play with the notion of remote presence through other people's sensory apparati—a primitive kind of simstim (a concept introduced by William Gibson in *Neuromancer*).

their work, unmediated by journalists or other interpreters. In that way the emerging medium is being more directly and dynamically shaped by the culture at large. Perhaps the most exciting thing of all is that this global conversation is happening in the genuinely formative stages of the medium and not after the fact.

All new media begin with visions—fantasies, desires, and ideas about new kinds of experiences that people might have. As development progresses, these visions can be overshadowed by the more immediate concerns of technology development. Too often, the technological perspective comes to dominate not only the process of development, but also the shape of the emerging medium itself. The visionary impulse fades away as technological progress becomes the sole focus. Some of the powers that a medium might have had are lost in the rush to find near-term solutions. Likewise, early successes with specific applications for new media can arrest growth and limit future potential by funneling resources into areas of development that seem most likely to provide the greatest short-term profit. The state of the art in computer games and commercial television are examples of these phenomena.

A counter-example is film. So many of the key elements of cinematic form and technique were invented by D. W. Griffith that we are tempted to think that the medium sprang full-blown from his brow. But Griffith's quantum leaps were preceded both by the development of some baseline technological capabilities that allowed him to envision the form and by experiments in which other artists sought the shape of the new medium in comparisons with its predecessors, most notably the stage. The recapitulation of previous forms seems to be as intrinsic to the evolution of media as it is to the development of human individuals in the womb: Human embryos have gills and tails before they assume uniquely human shape; television emulated theatre, vaudeville, radio, and film. The emergence of a new medium is a dance between the evolutionary pattern or recapitulation and the force of new creative visions.

The new literature of virtual reality includes some excellent examples of the kinds of experiences people might have with such systems and the kinds of uses to which they might be put. Both Fisher [1990] and Lanier [Heilbrun, 1989] describe surgical simulators for the training of physicians, for instance. The miracles of scale transformation can enable engineers to adjust the angles of airplane wings with their (gloved) hands and chip designers to walk around inside their microcircuits. Here, the materials can be taken more or less directly from real life, and the action (unless a nurse is handing you a scalpel) can be supplied by the single human agent. But applications in art, entertainment, and education require simulations of more than the physical aspects of a world; those who want to learn, play, and dream in the Holodeck will have to wait for a system that can sustain characters and orchestrate action (Color Plate XI). Judging from the accelerating pace of research and development, they may not have to wait too long.

At Ars Electronica, an international conference on computer-based art held in Linz, Austria, in September 1990, a slogan was introduced: "The future goes to virtual reality."[8] This slogan suggests that virtual reality is more than a new form of human-computer activity; rather it may be a new stage in the evolution of interactive media. The diversity of applications that have been envisioned for it suggests that virtual-reality technology has the potential to be pervasive and to enhance our ability to take action in a wide variety of representational contexts. As the field of virtual reality has coalesced over the last ten years, it has seemed more and more to me like Pygmalion's statue. Those of us who have been involved in the process have nudged the medium in the direction of our own visions of human-computer symbiosis, but we have also been alternatively delighted and vexed by the ways in which the medium has taken on a life of its own.

In a hopeful vein, it is important to notice that new media open new possibilities for experience. Surely, virtual reality

---

[8]The odd syntax is probably an artifact of translation.

will contain more than databases and games. To close the circle from an artistic perspective, I want to describe one vision of what virtual reality systems might be able to provide for us. The goals of consciousness expansion, personal liberation, and the transformation of one's relationship to the world may seem lofty in relation to the little boxes we have on our desks today, but they are at the heart of the purpose of art. Critics of virtual reality warn that technology-based "psychedelics" will produce a disembodied race, a culture that ceases to value the body, nature, or physical reality in general because the alternative will be so persuasive. I believe that the reverse is true.

I want to illustrate this point with a personal parable. During the summer of 1990, I spent some time exploring ruins of the Anasazi civilization in New Mexico and Arizona with a knowledgeable guide. We pondered petroglyphs—ancient carvings in rocks—in the environs of Santa Fe, in the ruins of a mesa-top city called Tsiping in Chaco Canyon, and finally at the Grand Canyon, the spiritual center of the universe for the Anasazi people (Color Plate XII). As we traveled throughout the Southwest, my companions and I became increasingly aware of the psychedelic shapes and textures of the rocks themselves. As shadows paraded across canyon walls, faces and forms would emerge and fade, leaving us finally unable to determine which were the works of human craftsmen and which were the result of the spontaneous collaboration of our own imaginations with the landscape.

Depicted in the petroglyphs were animals, spirit beings, and the symbolic spiral that represented the Anasazi view of the nature of time, the story of origins, and the fundamental shape of being. Our guide showed us how many of the carvings had apparently begun with some contour in the rock itself—the suggestion of a leg, a curling tail, a brow. "The makers of these carvings revealed the faces of the spirits that lived in the rocks," he explained. We readily believed. I thought of the ancient Greek idea that inside every piece of marble is a perfect sculpture, and that it is the humble job of the artist to reveal it and not to superimpose some form of his own imagining on the substance. But now the principle had a new and deeper resonance. Both petroglyphs and sculptures articulate the essential relationship between the human spirit and the physical world.

Art is time travel; it transmits understanding across time and space. Carvings and sculptures, houses and temples, plays and symphonies are asynchronous conversations between the makers of a work and those who experience it. But the *experience* of art is in the here and now. Realtime is where the conversation takes place and where illumination is achieved. In this way, art itself is "telepresence." From the plays of ancient Greece to the ritual dances of the Anasazi to the concerts of the Grateful Dead, realtime experience is the Dionysian dimension of art. Recall that in the Greek theatre, actors were the priests of Dionysus, the god of ecstasy and rebirth, and during the act of performance they felt themselves to be *in possession of the god.* Their audiences were transported and illuminated by the divine presence. Dionysian experience is the experience of being *in the living presence* of not only the artist but also huge spiritual forces.

I think we can someday have Dionysian experiences in virtual reality, and that they will be experiences of the most intimate and powerful kind. But to do so we must breathe life into our tools. Our creative force must be manifest, not as an *artifact* but as a *collaborator*—an extension of ourselves embodied in our systems. There must be more behind the looking glass than a room that one steps into, and there must be more to virtual reality than the engineering of the looking glass.

For virtual reality to succeed in meeting these goals, we need continual and deep involvement by artists in the ongoing process of understanding what virtual reality is for and what it can be. We need convivial tools that allow artists to work in the medium in order to influence its evolution. Most of all, we need artists to help us understand how virtual reality, like other art forms, can inform and enrich human experience.

At the height of the Anasazi civilization in the great kivas, humans enacted spirits and gods. Long before these magical presences emerged from the shadows, dancing would begin on huge foot-drums whose throbbing could be heard a hundred miles away across the desert. The experience was an altered state that culminated in the performance in the living presence [see Rheingold, 1991]. The great kivas are silent today (Color Plate XIII). Even in our magnificent cathedrals, we hear only echoes of a magnitude of experience that has faded from our lives. There are no magical meeting places at the center of our culture, no sacred circles inside of which all that one does has a heightened significance. In those few places where such transformations can still occur, the shadow of our civilization is fast obliterating the possibility.

What happens when one steps inside the magic circle? The meaning of the ordinary is transformed. Back in the early 1970s, I wrote (with William Morton) and directed a play about Robin Hood. The stories we used were among the earliest, and they were quite strange and primal in comparison with the more familiar romantic versions of the myth. The audience gathered below an old gothic tower near a lake. We used medieval mansion-style staging for the performance. Suddenly, a minstrel appeared and began to sing. She invited the audience to follow her into the woods, where they would come upon different scenes unfolding in various locales around the lake. My clearest memory is of the reaction of a little boy as the play began. The minstrel appeared and announced that this was Sherwood Forest. I watched the boy take hold of a nearby branch and gaze with awe at an ordinary oak leaf. "This is Sherwood Forest," he whispered, and I believe he really *looked* at an oak leaf for the first time in his life.

Virtual reality may be many things. It may become a tool, a game machine, or just a mutant form of TV. But for virtual reality to fulfill its highest potential, we must reinvent the sacred spaces where we collaborate with reality in order to transform it and ourselves.

With virtual-reality systems, the future is quite literally within our grasp. The dimension of enactment has undergone a rapid, qualitative transformation in the last decade. The challenge for the next decade is to arrive at understandings and technologies that can bring the other dimensions of human-computer experience to the same level. At the point of parity, synergy will kick in. Perhaps more important than technology development is the need to recognize our new opposable thumb for what it is. Like every qualitatively new human capability before it, the ability to represent new worlds in which humans can learn, explore, and act will blow a hole in all our old imaginings and expectations. Through that hole we can glimpse a world of which both cause and effect are a quantum leap in human evolution.

# References


Agre, Philip E. "The Dynamic Structure of Everyday Life." Ph.D. diss., Massachusetts Institute of Technology, 1988.

Allen, Gay Wilson, and Harry Hayden Clark, eds. *Literary Criticism: Pope to Croce*. Detroit: Wayne State University Press, 1962.

Apple Computer, Inc. *Apple Human Interface Guidelines: The Apple Desktop Interface*. Reading, Mass.: Addison-Wesley, 1987.

Aristotle, *The Poetics*. Translated by Ingram Bywater. In *Rhetoric and Poetics of Aristotle*. Edited by Friedrich Solmsen. New York: The Modern Library, 1954.

Baecker, Ronald M., and William A. S. Buxton. *Readings in Human-Computer Interaction: A Multidisciplinary Approach*. Los Altos, Calif.: Morgan Kauffmann Publishers, 1987.

Bates, Joseph. "Computational Drama in Oz." Working notes of the AAAI Workshop on Interactive Fiction and Synthetic Realities, Boston, July 1990. Available from School of Computer Science, Carnegie Mellon University, Pittsburgh, Pa.

Bender, Tom. *Environmental Design Primer*. Minneapolis: Published by author, 1973.

Bødker, Sussane. "A Human Activity Approach to User Interfaces." *Human-Computer Interaction*, 4 (1989): 171–195.

Bødker, Sussane. *Through the Interface: A Human Activity Approach to User Interface Design*. Hillsdale, N.J.: Lawrence Erlbaum, 1990.

Bradbury, Ray. "The Murderer." In *The Golden Apples of the Sun*, Doubleday, Garden City, NY, 1953.

Brand, Stewart. *II Cybernetic Frontiers*. New York: Random House and Berkeley, CA: The Bookworks, 1974.

Brecht, Bertolt. *Brecht on Theatre*. Translated by John Willett. New York, 1964.

Brennan, Susan E. "Conversation as Direct Manipulation: An Iconoclastic View." In *The Art of Human-Computer Interface Design*, edited by Brenda Laurel. Reading, Mass.: Addison-Wesley, 1990a.

Brennan, Susan E., "Seeking and Providing Evidence for Mutual Understanding." Ph.D. diss., Stanford University, 1990b.

Brockett, Oscar G. *History of the Theatre*. Boston: Allyn and Bacon, 1968.

Brown, John Seely. "From Cognitive to Social Ergonomics. In *User Centered System Design: New Perspectives on Human-Computer Interaction*, edited by D.A. Norman and S. Draper. Hillsdale, NJ: Lawrence Erlbaum, 1986.

Buxton, William. "The 'Natural' Language of Interaction: A Perspective on Non-Verbal Dialogues." In *The Art of Human-Computer Interface Design*, edited by Brenda Laurel. Reading, Mass.: Addison-Wesley, 1990.

Carbonell, Jaime G. "Towards a Process Model of Human Personality Traits," *Artificial Intelligence* 15 (1980): 49–50.

Chekhov, Michael. *To the Actor: On the Technique of Acting*. New York: Harper and Row, 1953.

Chew, Frederick F. "Beneath the Surface of NewWave Office." *HP Professional*, vol. 4, no. 4 (April 1990): 44–53.

Clark, Herbert H., and Susan E. Brennan, "Grounding in Communication." In *Socially Shared Cognition*, edited by L. B. Resnick, J. Levine, and S. D. Behrend, American Psychological Association, 1990.

Clark, H. H., and T. Carlson, "Hearers and Speech Acts." *Language* 58 (2) (1982) 332–373.

Clark, H. H., and C. R. Marshall, "Definite Reference and Mutual Knowledge." In *Elements of Discourse Understanding*, edited by A. K. Joshi, B. L. Webber, and I. A. Sag, Cambridge, England: Cambridge University Press, 1981.

Clynes, Manfred. *Sentics: The Touch of Emotions*. Garden City, N.Y.: Anchor Press, 1977.

Crawford, Chris. "Lessons from Computer Game Design." In *The Art of Human-Computer Interface Design*, edited by Brenda Laurel. Reading, Mass.: Addison-Wesley, 1990.

Crowston, Kevin, and Thomas W. Malone. "Intelligent Software Agents," *Byte* 13:13 (December 1988): 267–274.

Cypher, Allen. "Managing the Mundane." In *The Art of Human-Computer Interface Design*, edited by Brenda Laurel. Reading, Mass.: Addison-Wesley, 1990.

Cypher, Allen. "Eager: Programming Repetitive Tasks by Example." Submitted for publication to *Proceedings of the CHI '91 Conference on Human Factors in Computing Systems*, New Orleans, April 28–May 2, 1991. New York: Association for Computing Machinery.

Don, Abbe. "Narrative and the Interface." In *The Art of Human-Computer Interface Design*, edited by Brenda Laurel. Reading, Mass.: Addison-Wesley, 1990.

Dyer, Michael G. *In-Depth Understanding: A Computer Model of Integrated Processing for Narrative Comprehension.* Cambridge, Mass.: The MIT Press, 1983.

Erickson, Tom. "Working with Interface Metaphors." In *The Art of Human-Computer Interface Design*, edited by Brenda Laurel. Reading, Mass.: Addison-Wesley, 1990.

Fast, Julius. *Body Language.* New York: Pocket Books, 1971.

Finzer, William, and Laura Gould. "Programming by Rehearsal." *Byte* (June 1984): 187–210.

Fisher, Scott S. "Virtual Reality Systems." In *The Art of Human-Computer Interface Design*, edited by Brenda Laurel. Reading, Mass.: Addison-Wesley, 1990.

Freytag, Gustav. *Technique of the Drama*, 2d ed. Translated by Elias J. MacEwan. Chicago: Scott, Foresman, 1898.

Gallwey, W. Timothy. *Inner Tennis: Playing the Game.* New York: Random House, 1976.

Gaver, William W. "The SonicFinder, an Interface That Uses Auditory Icons." *Human Machine Interaction*, 4 (1989).

Gaver, William W., and Randall B. Smith. "Auditory Icons in Large-Scale Collaborative Environments." In *Human-Computer Interaction—Interact '90*, edited by D. Diaper. Elsevier, North-Holland.

Gilbert, Ron. "Why Adventure Games Suck." *The Journal of Computer Game Design*, vol. 3, no. 2 (December 1989): 4–7.

Hartnoll, Phyllis, ed. *The Oxford Companion to the Theatre.* 3rd ed. London: Oxford University Press, 1967.

Heckell, Paul. *The Elements of Friendly Software design.* New York: Warner Books, 1982.

Heilbrun, Adam. "Virtual Reality: An Interview with Jaron Lanier." *Whole Earth Review,* 64 (Fall 1989): 108–119.

Hilton, Julian. "Some Semiotic Reflections on the Future of Artificial Intelligence." In *Artificial Intelligence: Future, Impacts, Challenges,* edited by R. Trappl. New York: Hemisphere, forthcoming.

Horowitz, Ellis. "An Integrated System for Creating Educational Software," vol. 8, no. 1 (Spring 1988): 35–42.

Hovy, Eduard H. *Generating Natural Language under Pragmatic Constraints.* Hillsdale, N.J.: Lawrence Erlbaum, 1988.

Hovy, Eduard H. "Pragmatics and Language Generation." *AI Journal,* forthcoming [1990].

Hutchins, Edwin L., James D. Hollan, and Donald A. Norman. "Direct Manipulation Interfaces." In *User Centered System Design: New Perspectives on Human-Computer Interaction,* edited by D.A. Norman and S. Draper. Hillsdale, NJ: Lawrence Erlbaum, 1986.

Kantrowitz, Mark. "GLINDA: Natural Language Text Generation in the Oz Interactive Fiction Project." CMU-CS-90-158, Carnegie Mellon University School of Computer Science, July 1990.

Karimi, Shay, Brenda Laurel, Tim Oren, and Abbe Don. *Evaluating Guides: A User Testing Study.* Apple Computer Technical Report, 1989.

Kay, Alan. "Computer Software." *Scientific American,* vol. 251, no. 3 (September 1984): 52–59.

Kitto, H. D. F. "Aristotle." In *The Oxford Companion to the Theatre,* 3rd ed., edited by Phyllis Hartnoll. London: Oxford University Press, 1967.

Krueger, Myron. "VIDEOPLACE and the Interface of the Future." In *The Art of Human-Computer Interface Design,* edited by Brenda Laurel. Reading, Mass.: Addison-Wesley, 1990.

Kurtenbach, Gordon, and Eric Hulteen. "Gestures in Human-Computer Interaction." In *The Art of Human-Computer Interface Design*, edited by Brenda Laurel. Reading, Mass.: Addison-Wesley, 1990.

Lakoff, George, and Mark Johnson. *Metaphors We Live By.* Chicago and London: University of Chicago Press, 1980.

Laurel, Brenda. "Toward the Design of a Computer-Based Interactive Fantasy System." Ph.D. diss., The Ohio State University, 1986a.

Laurel, Brenda. "Interface as Mimesis." In *User Centered System Design: New Perspectives on Human-Computer Interaction*, edited by D.A. Norman and S. Draper. Hillsdale, NJ: Lawrence Erlbaum, 1986b.

Laurel, Brenda. "Interface Agents as Dramatic Characters." Presentation for panel, "Drama and Personality in Interface Design." *Proceedings of CHI '89*, ACM SIGCHI, Austin, Tex., May, 1989.

Laurel, Brenda, Tim Oren, and Abbe Don. "Issues in Multimedia Interface Design: Media Integration and Interface Agents." *Proceedings of CHI '90*, ACM SIGCHI, April 1990.

Laurel, Brenda. "Interface Agents: Metaphors with Character." In *The Art of Human-Computer Interface Design*, edited by Brenda Laurel. Reading, Mass.: Addison-Wesley, 1990.

Lebowitz, Michael. "Creating Characters in a Story-Telling Universe." *Poetics* 13 (1984):171–194.

Lehnert, Wendy Grace. "The Process of Question Answering." Ph.D. diss., Yale University, 1977.

Lewis, D. K. *Convention: A Philosophical Study.* Cambridge, Mass.: Harvard University Press, 1969.

Malone, Thomas Wendell. "What Makes Things Fun to Learn? A Study of Intrinsically Motivating Computer Games." Ph.D. diss., Stanford University, 1980.

MacKay, D. M. "The Use of Behavioral Language to refer to Mechanical Processes." *British Journal of Philosophical Science*, vol. 13 (1962): 89–103.

May, Rollo. *The Courage to Create*. New York: W. W. Norton, 1975.

Meehan, James Richard. "The Metanovel: Writing Stories by Computer." Ph.D. diss., Yale University, 1976.

Minsky, Margaret R. "Manipulating Simulated Objects with Real-World Gestures Using a Force and Position Sensitive Screen," *SIGGRAPH '84 Conference Proceedings* (New York: ACM, 1984): 195–203.

Minsky, Margaret R., Ouh-young Ming, Oliver Steele, Frederick P. Brooks Jr., and Max Benhensky. "Feeling and Seeing: Issues in Force Display." *Computer Graphics,* vol. 24, no. 2 (March 1990).

Negroponte, Nicholas. "Hospital Corners." In *The Art of Human-Computer Interface Design,* edited by Brenda Laurel. Reading, Mass.: Addison-Wesley, 1990.

Nelson, Theodor Holm. "Getting It Out of Our System." In *Information Retrieval: A Critical View,* edited by George Schecter. Philadelphia, Penn.: Frankford Arsenal, 1967.

Nelson, Theodor Holm. "The Right Way to Think about Software Design." In *The Art of Human-Computer Interface Design* edited by Brenda Laurel. Reading, Mass.: Addison-Wesley, 1990.

Norman, Donald A., and S. Draper, eds., *User Centered System Design: New Perspectives on Human-Computer Interaction.* Hillsdale, N.J.: Lawrence Erlbaum, 1986.

Norman, Donald A. *The Psychology of Everyday Things.* New York: Basic Books, 1988.

Norman, Donald A. "Cognitive Artifacts." Department of Cognitive Science, University of California, San Diego, 1990. To be published in a book edited by John M. Carroll.

Ong, Walter. *Orality and Literacy: The Technologizing of the Word.* London: Methuen, 1982.

Owen, David. "Naive Theories of Computation." In *User Centered System Design: New Perspectives on Human-Computer Interaction,* edited by D.A. Norman and S. Draper. Hillsdale, NJ: Lawrence Erlbaum, 1986.

Rand, Ayn. *Night of January 16th.* New York: The World Publishing Company, 1988.

Rheingold, Howard. "What's the Big Deal about Cyberspace?" In *The Art of Human-Computer Interface Design,* edited by Brenda Laurel. Reading, Mass.: Addison-Wesley, 1990.

Rheingold, Howard. *Exploring the World of Virtual Reality.* Simon and Schuster, forthcoming.

Rosen, Joseph, and Mort Grosser. "Nerve Repair at the Axon Level —A Merger of Microsurgery and Microelectronics." *Artificial Organs,* edited by J. Andrade. New York: VCH Publishers, 1987: 583–594.

Rubinstein, Richard, and Harry Hersch. *The Human Factor: Designing Computer Systems for People.* Digital Press, 1984.

Sado, Katsumi. "The TRON House Comes to Tokyo." *Byte Magazine,* April 1990, p. 33.

Salomon, Gitta."Designing Causal-Use Hypertext: The CHI '89 Info Booth." *Proceedings of CHI '90.* Seattle, Wash. (April 1990): 451–458.

Schank, Roger C., and Michael Lebowitz. "The Use of Stereotype Information in the Comprehension of Noun Phrases." Alexandria, Va.: Defense Technical Information Center, 1979.

Schelling, T. C. *The Strategy of Conflict.* Oxford, England: Oxford University Press, 1960.

Schmandt, Chris, and Barry Arons. "Phone Slave: A Graphical Telecommunications Interface." *Proc. of the Soc. for Information Display,* 26(1):79 (1985):82.

Schmandt, Chris. "Understanding Speech Without Recognizing Words." *Proceedings of the American Voice Input/Output Society,* 1987.

Schmandt, Chris. "Illusion in the Interface." In *The Art of Human-Computer Interface Design,* edited by Brenda Laurel. Reading, Mass.: Addison-Wesley, 1990.

Schmandt, C. M., and E. A. Hulteen. "The Intelligent Voice-Interactive Interface." *Proceedings of Human Factors in Computing Systems.* (March 1982): 363–366.

Schwamberger, Jeffrey. "The Nature of Dramatic Character." Ph.D. diss., The Ohio State University, 1980.

Shneiderman, Ben. "The Future of Interactive Systems and the Emergence of Direct Manipulation." *Behavior and Information Technology,* I (1982): 237–256.

Shneiderman, Ben. *Designing the User Interface: Strategies for Effective Human-Computer Interaction*. Reading, Mass.: Addison-Wesley, 1987.

Shneiderman, Ben. "A Nonanthropomorphic Style Guide: Overcoming the Humpty Dumpty Syndrome." *The Computing Teacher* (October 1988): 9–10.

Smiley, Sam. *Playwriting: The Structure of Action*. Englewood Cliffs, N.J.: Prentice-Hall, 1971.

Stebbins, Geneviève. *Delsarte System of Dramatic Expression*. New York: E. S. Werner, 1886.

Suchman, Lucy A. *Plans and Situated Actions: The Problem of Human-Machine Communication*. Cambridge: Cambridge University Press, 1987.

Sussman, Vic. "Home Smart Home." *Washington Post Magazine* (January 10, 1988): w45.

Sutherland, Ivan E. "Sketchpad: A Man-Machine Graphical Communication System." *Proceedings of the Spring Joint Computer Conference* (1963): 329–346.

Turkle, Sherry. *The Second Self: Computers and the Human Spirit*. New York: Simon and Schuster, 1984.

Turner, Scott. "MINSTREL: A Model of Storytelling and Creativity." Technical Note UCLA-AI-N-90-10, Artificial Intelligence Laboratory, Computer Science Department, University of California, Los Angeles, 1990.

Vinge, Vernor. "True Names." In *Binary Star No. 5*, edited by James R. Frenkel. New York: Dell Publishing, 1981.

Walker, John. "Through the Looking Glass." In *The Art of Human-Computer Interface Design*, edited by Brenda Laurel. Reading, Mass.: Addison-Wesley, 1990.

# Index

## Index

# Index